The Future of Work

How Remote Work Automation and the Gig Economy Are Shaping Careers and Industries

Table of Contents

Introduction 1

Chapter 1 The Evolution of Work 4

    From the Industrial Age to the Digital Revolution 5

    The Shift in Work Structures Over Decades 7

    The Rise of Knowledge-Based Economies 9

Chapter 2 The Remote Work Revolution 12

    Remote Work Before and After the Pandemic 13

    Benefits for Employers and Employees 15

    Tools and Technologies Enabling Remote Work 17

Chapter 3 Automation and AI in the Workforce 20

    What is Automation and How Does It Work? 21

    Industries Most Affected by AI and Robotics 23

    The Future of Human-AI Collaboration 26

Chapter 4 The Rise of the Gig Economy 28

    The Growth of Freelancing and Contract Work 29

    Platforms Empowering the Gig Economy 31

    The Pros and Cons of Gig Work 33

Chapter 5 The Digital Nomad Lifestyle 36

The Rise of Location-Independent Careers 37

Managing Work and Travel Simultaneously 39

The Tools and Technologies for Digital Nomads 41

Chapter 6 Reskilling and Up-skilling for the Future 44

Why Lifelong Learning is Essential 45

Key Skills for the Future Job Market 47

How to Find the Right Learning Opportunities 49

Chapter 7 Technology Shaping the Future of Work 52

The Impact of Artificial Intelligence 53

Blockchain and Its Potential in Employment 55

How Automation Will Redefine Jobs 57

Chapter 8 Technology Shaping the Future of Work 60

The Impact of Artificial Intelligence 61

Blockchain and Its Potential in Employment 64

How Automation Will Redefine Jobs 65

Chapter 9 Redefining Job Security 68

Moving Away from Traditional Job Models 69

Building Stability in the Gig Economy 71

Financial Security and Health Benefits for Gig Workers 73

Chapter 10 Leadership in a Remote World 76

Managing Remote Teams Effectively 77

Building a Strong Company Culture Online 79

Overcoming Communication Barriers in Virtual Teams 81

Chapter 11 The Impact of Automation on Employment 84

Which Jobs Are at Risk of Being Automated? 85

The Potential for New Job Roles in an Automated World 87

Strategies for Adapting to Automation 89

Chapter 12 Ethics and Regulation in the Future of Work ... 92

The Ethical Implications of AI and Automation 93

Legal Issues Surrounding Gig Work 96

Government Policies for Protecting Workers in the Future 98

Introduction

The world of work is undergoing a profound transformation, driven by rapid technological advancements, shifting societal expectations, and evolving global economies. As the landscape of work continues to evolve, the traditional concepts of employment, career paths, and the workplace itself are being redefined. In this new era, the rise of remote work, automation, and the gig economy are central forces reshaping how we live, work, and interact with our professional environments.

In recent decades, the workforce has seen a dramatic shift. The rigid 9-to-5 office jobs that once defined the majority of careers are being replaced by more flexible, dynamic forms of employment. The COVID-19 pandemic, in particular, catalyzed the widespread adoption of remote work, which has now become a staple for millions of workers worldwide. The digital revolution has made it possible for people to collaborate, communicate, and contribute to global projects from virtually anywhere. This shift is not merely about location; it also reflects a larger change in the way businesses operate and how employees engage with their work.

The modern workforce is more diverse than ever before, with a growing number of individuals pursuing non-traditional career paths, such as freelancing, contracting, and part-time work. Traditional employment models are increasingly being replaced by a new paradigm where workers are not just employees but also entrepreneurs, managing their time, skills, and income in increasingly flexible and innovative ways. The rise of the gig economy and freelance platforms such as Uber, Fiverr, and Upwork is a testament to this shift, where individuals can pursue a variety of opportunities without being bound by the constraints of a traditional job.

Several key factors are driving this transformation. Technology, particularly automation and artificial intelligence (AI), has fundamentally changed the way businesses operate and the types of skills that are in demand. Machines are now capable of performing tasks that once required human labor, leading to increased efficiency and productivity in industries like manufacturing, logistics, and customer service. While automation offers significant economic benefits, it also raises concerns about job displacement and the need for workers to adapt to new technologies.

Alongside automation, the proliferation of digital tools and platforms has made remote work not only possible but efficient. The rise of cloud computing, project management software, and communication tools like Zoom and Slack have enabled businesses to operate with distributed teams. Remote work, which was once seen as a niche or temporary arrangement, has become a mainstream mode of operation, with many companies adopting hybrid or fully remote workforces.

Finally, the gig economy is another significant driver of change. As more people seek flexibility and independence, platforms that connect freelancers with clients have surged in popularity. These platforms allow individuals to leverage their skills in a more autonomous way, creating an economy where people are no longer tied to a single employer or job. This shift also challenges traditional labor laws and regulations, as gig workers often face uncertainty when it comes to benefits, job security, and income stability.

Looking ahead, the future of work promises to be shaped by continued technological advances, societal changes, and the ongoing integration of automation into daily business operations. The jobs of tomorrow may not look anything like those of today. Some existing roles will be replaced by machines, while entirely new industries and career paths will emerge. To thrive in this new landscape, workers will need to be adaptable, continually learning, and prepared to embrace new opportunities in a rapidly changing world.

The future of work will require a shift in mindset, where workers prioritize skills over traditional job titles, and businesses focus on flexibility and adaptability rather than rigid employment structures. As remote work, automation, and the gig economy continue to influence the workforce, the key to success will lie in one's ability to navigate and leverage these changes. Embracing these transformations is not just about surviving the future of work; it's about thriving in it.

Chapter 1
The Evolution of Work

The story of work begins in the mills and factories of the Industrial Age, where steam engines and assembly lines first replaced handcraftsmanship and small-scale production. Entire communities grew around factories, and people's lives were organized around strict schedules and standardized tasks. The transformation that began in the late 18th century depended on mechanization—machines powered by coal and steam that could perform heavy labor more quickly and cheaply than human workers. As transport and communication networks expanded, goods and services could move farther and faster, creating new markets and redefining what it meant to earn a living.

Over the decades, work structures evolved in response to each wave of technological innovation. Electricity and the internal combustion engine ushered in mass production and the automotive age. The mid-20th century brought computers, enabling unprecedented data processing and office automation. With each shift, job roles expanded beyond manual labor into technical, managerial, and clerical positions. Organizational hierarchies became taller and more complex, and careers were often defined by long-term tenure with a single employer.

Today, we find ourselves in the midst of the Digital Revolution. The internet, mobile computing, and cloud technologies have dismantled many of the old boundaries of work. Tasks that once required specialized physical infrastructure can now be performed anywhere there is a connection. Information and knowledge have become the most valuable commodities, leading to the rise of knowledge-based economies. In these economies, intellectual capital—creativity, problem-solving, and specialized expertise—drives innovation and growth. Industries such as software development, digital marketing, and biotech exemplify this shift, placing a premium on continuous learning and adaptability.

As work continues to evolve, understanding its journey from the Industrial Age through successive revolutions helps us anticipate future changes. What began with coal-fired machines and rigid factories has led to flexible digital platforms and decentralized teams. The challenge now is to harness the power of knowledge, technology, and human ingenuity to create work that is not only efficient and productive but also meaningful and sustainable.

From the Industrial Age to the Digital Revolution

The transition from the Industrial Age to the Digital Revolution represents one of the most profound shifts in human history, fundamentally transforming economies, societies, and the nature of work. The Industrial Age, which began in the late 18th century, was driven by mechanization: steam engines, water power, and later, coal-fired factories enabled mass production and standardized manufacturing. Assembly lines, epitomized by Henry Ford's automotive plants in the early 20th century, optimized efficiency by breaking complex jobs into simple, repeatable tasks. Labor became more specialized, schedules more regimented, and workers often found themselves tethered to a single employer for decades. Urbanization accelerated as people left agrarian lives to seek factory employment, giving rise to new social dynamics and labor movements demanding fair wages and safer conditions.

Electricity and the internal combustion engine further accelerated change. Factories no longer needed to be sited next to rivers; they could locate wherever power lines and roads reached. Production scaled up, global trade networks expanded, and consumer goods flooded markets. During this period, white-collar jobs grew: clerical work, management, and technical professions emerged to support complex organizational structures. Education systems adapted, emphasizing literacy, numeracy, and vocational skills tailored to industrial needs.

By the mid-20th century, electronic computers began to appear. Early machines like ENIAC were room-sized and task-specific, yet they hinted at a new era. As computing hardware shrank and costs dropped, businesses adopted computers for data processing, inventory control, and payroll—tasks once handled by armies of typists and bookkeepers. The 1970s and '80s saw personal computers and local area networks transform offices into digital hubs. Software suites automated many routine functions, and organizations restructured to leverage this newfound flexibility.

The true inflection point came with the birth of the internet and mobile technologies in the 1990s and early 2000s. The World Wide Web democratized information access; email and VoIP dissolved geographic barriers, enabling collaboration across continents. Cloud computing liberated data and applications from on-premise servers, allowing teams to work from anywhere—in essence, the first real "remote work" environments. As bandwidth increased and mobile devices proliferated, the workplace became untethered from the office. Gigabytes replaced blueprints, digital platforms supplanted storefronts, and value migrated from physical capital to intellectual property and data.

Today's knowledge-based economy rewards creativity, problem-solving, and adaptability. Jobs once considered secure—manufacturing line operators, data entry clerks—have been automated or outsourced, while demand surges for software developers, data scientists, and digital marketers. Continuous learning is now essential; workers must evolve alongside technology. The journey from steam engines to smartphones underscores a perpetual cycle of innovation, challenging us to reimagine work not as a location or a rigid set of tasks, but as a dynamic interplay between human ingenuity and technological capability.

The Shift in Work Structures Over Decades

Over the course of the twentieth and twenty-first centuries, work structures have undergone remarkable transformations in response to technological innovation, economic pressures, and cultural shifts. In the early twentieth century, factories and offices were organized around rigid hierarchies and clearly defined roles. Workers arrived punctually each day, performed narrowly specialized tasks, and reported to a chain of command that emphasized control and predictability. This model valued efficiency in mass production and consistency in administrative processes, but it often stifled creativity and constrained individual autonomy.

By mid-century, white-collar employment expanded rapidly. Large corporations built layered bureaucracies to manage growing workforces. Departments multiplied, each with its own managers and protocols. Career paths tended to follow a linear progression, rewarding loyalty and tenure above all. Many employees expected to spend decades at a single company, climbing the corporate ladder in exchange for job security and benefits. At the same time, office environments relied on centralized decision-making; information flowed upward and directives flowed downward, reinforcing a command-and-control paradigm.

With the arrival of computers and the internet in the 1980s and 1990s, organizations began to rethink this model. Information became easier to share, and teams could collaborate across locations. Companies experimented with flatter structures, reducing layers of management to speed decision-making and encourage cross-functional cooperation. The concept of project-based work gained traction: instead of permanent departments, firms formed temporary teams that dissolved upon completion. This shift enabled greater flexibility, but it also introduced challenges in coordination and accountability.

In the early 2000s, agile methodologies borrowed from software development further reshaped work structures. Agile teams prioritized rapid iteration, self-organization, and continuous feedback. Roles became fluid: product owners, scrum masters, and development teams worked in short cycles to deliver incremental value. This approach spread beyond technology into marketing, finance, and even operations, fostering a culture of experimentation and learning. Physical spaces evolved as well: open-plan offices, hot-desking, and coworking encouraged spontaneous interaction and broke down silos.

Most recently, the COVID-19 pandemic accelerated the shift toward hybrid and fully remote models. Employers adopted cloud tools, video conferencing, and asynchronous communication to support distributed teams. Trust replaced constant supervision as the primary means of ensuring productivity. Meanwhile, the rise of freelance and gig platforms has created a parallel labor market where individuals choose their own assignments, schedules, and clients. Gig workers juggle multiple projects, leveraging digital marketplaces to market specialized skills.

Today's work structures blend traditional and emergent elements. Many organizations embrace hybrid hierarchies: core teams maintain stability, while dynamic pods form to tackle new initiatives. Performance metrics emphasize outcomes over hours logged. Continuous learning and adaptability have become central to career success, as employees navigate shifting expectations and rapidly evolving technologies. This ongoing evolution reflects a fundamental reimagining of work itself—from a static arrangement of roles and tasks to a fluid ecosystem defined by collaboration, autonomy, and the endless pursuit of innovation.

The Rise of Knowledge-Based Economies

Over the past several decades, economies around the world have shifted from being driven primarily by natural resources and manufacturing to being powered by knowledge, innovation, and intellectual capital. This transformation—often called the rise of knowledge-based economies—reflects the growing importance of information, technology, and human creativity as the key drivers of growth, competitiveness, and prosperity.

In knowledge-based economies, value is created less by the extraction of raw materials or assembly of goods and more by the generation, dissemination, and application of ideas. Industries such as software development, biotechnology, finance, education, and creative services have become cornerstones of economic activity. Companies invest heavily in research and development, data analytics, and digital platforms in order to differentiate their offerings and maintain competitive advantage. Patents, copyrights, and trade secrets have risen in importance, and intellectual property laws play a critical role in protecting and incentivizing innovation.

Education and lifelong learning are central to success in these economies. Workers need not only foundational knowledge but also advanced skills in critical thinking, problem solving, and collaboration. Universities, vocational schools, and online learning platforms have adapted by offering specialized programs in data science, artificial intelligence, renewable energy, and other emerging fields. Governments and private organizations often partner to create innovation hubs, technology parks, and incubators where startups and researchers can collaborate, access funding, and bring new ideas to market.

Digital infrastructure underpins the knowledge economy. High-speed internet, cloud computing, and mobile connectivity enable the rapid exchange of information and seamless collaboration across borders. Firms leverage big data and machine learning to identify market trends, optimize operations, and personalize customer experiences. At the same time, this connectivity introduces challenges related to cybersecurity, data privacy, and digital inequality; policymakers and businesses must work together to ensure that the benefits of the knowledge economy are broadly shared.

The rise of knowledge-based economies has also reshaped labor markets. Routine tasks in manufacturing and administration are increasingly automated, while demand grows for roles that require creativity, emotional intelligence, and complex cognitive skills. Freelancing and remote work have become more common as digital platforms connect skilled professionals with clients worldwide. Workers must therefore be adaptable, continuously updating their skill sets and personal brands to remain relevant.

Despite its many advantages, the knowledge economy raises questions about equity and social cohesion. Wage disparities can widen between highly skilled knowledge workers and those in traditional roles. Regions without strong educational institutions or digital infrastructure risk falling behind. Addressing these disparities requires coordinated investment in education, broadband access, and workforce development programs.

Ultimately, the rise of knowledge-based economies represents a profound realignment of what drives wealth and opportunity. By valuing human creativity, collaboration, and technological innovation above all else, societies can unleash new sources of growth. At the same time, they must navigate the complex challenges of inclusion, regulation, and continuous learning to ensure that everyone benefits from this transformation.

Chapter 2
The Remote Work Revolution

Remote work was a niche arrangement long before it became a global necessity. In its early days, remote positions were limited to freelancers, consultants, and a handful of forward-thinking companies willing to experiment with telecommuting. Employees often worked from home one day a week or logged in during travel, relying on basic email and phone calls to stay in touch. However, most organizations still centered around physical offices, believing that productivity and collaboration required in-person interaction.

The COVID-19 pandemic disrupted this model overnight, forcing businesses of all sizes to send entire workforces home. Companies scrambled to equip employees with laptops, secure VPNs, and video conferencing accounts. What began as an emergency measure quickly revealed unexpected advantages. Employers discovered cost savings on real estate and utilities, while employees found relief from long commutes and rigid schedules. Productivity in many sectors remained stable or even improved, challenging long-held assumptions about where and how work must get done.

For employees, remote work has translated into greater autonomy, improved work-life balance, and the freedom to live outside expensive urban centers. Without daily commutes, many have reclaimed hours for family, exercise, or creative pursuits. Employers, in turn, have gained access to a broader talent pool unrestricted by geography. Companies can tap specialists from around the world, reducing hiring bottlenecks and fostering more diverse teams. Remote work also supports business continuity — when local disruptions strike, teams can continue operations from anywhere.

Underpinning this revolution are a suite of powerful tools and technologies. Cloud collaboration platforms allow real-time co-editing of documents, while project management software tracks progress and deadlines. High-definition video conferencing bridges distance for team meetings and client presentations. Secure file-sharing services and encrypted communication channels protect sensitive data. Together, these innovations have not only enabled the mass adoption of remote work but also laid the foundation for hybrid models that blend the best of office and home environments. As these technologies evolve, the remote work revolution is poised to endure beyond any single crisis.

Remote Work Before and After the Pandemic

Remote work existed long before it became a global necessity, but it occupied a relatively small niche in most industries. In the 1980s and 1990s, telecommuting was heralded as a potential solution to traffic congestion and urban sprawl, and a handful of pioneering companies — often in technology or consulting — offered employees the option to work from home one or two days per week. These early arrangements relied heavily on dial-up internet connections, fax machines, and landline telephones. While telecommuters enjoyed reduced commutes and greater flexibility, many organizations remained skeptical, believing that productivity and collaboration suffered without in-person oversight. Remote work was often equated with part-time schedules, freelancing, or special accommodations for employees with unique needs.

By the early 2000s, improvements in broadband internet, virtual private networks (VPNs), and enterprise software made remote work more feasible. Cloud-based email and basic document-sharing platforms began to replace local servers, allowing team members to access files from outside the office. Yet even as these technologies matured, remote work adoption grew slowly. Cultural barriers remained strong: managers feared a loss of control, employees worried about career visibility, and office real estate was still viewed as essential for company identity. Surveys in the late 2010s consistently showed that fewer than 10 percent of U.S. workers had access to regular remote work options.

Everything changed in early 2020 when the COVID-19 pandemic forced organizations worldwide to shutter physical offices almost overnight. In mere weeks, businesses of all sizes scrambled to equip employees with laptops, secure VPNs, and collaboration tools. Video conferencing platforms like Zoom and Microsoft Teams experienced explosive growth, and companies rushed to formalize remote-work policies. What began as an emergency measure soon revealed unexpected benefits: many teams reported stable or even improved productivity, employees praised the elimination of lengthy commutes, and parents valued the flexibility to juggle work with home schooling and caregiving.

In the wake of this forced experiment, attitudes toward remote work shifted dramatically. By mid-2021, surveys showed that a majority of knowledge-economy workers preferred at least a hybrid model, combining days at home with days in the office. Employers recognized significant cost savings on real estate and utilities, and talent acquisition expanded beyond geographic constraints. At the same time, challenges emerged: "Zoom fatigue," blurred boundaries between work and personal life, and concerns around employee isolation and mental health. Today, many organizations are crafting hybrid structures—balancing remote autonomy with in-person collaboration—to capture the strengths of both models. The pandemic accelerated a long-term evolution, pushing remote work from a niche experiment to a defining feature of modern employment.

Benefits for Employers and Employees

Remote work offers a wealth of advantages that extend to both employers and employees, reshaping expectations around productivity, flexibility, and organizational culture. For employers, one of the most immediate benefits is cost savings. With fewer staff requiring dedicated office space, companies can downsize real estate footprints, reduce utilities expenses, and lower overhead costs related to office maintenance. These savings can be redirected into strategic investments—such as research and development, employee training, or technology upgrades—fueling long-term growth and innovation.

Access to a broader talent pool is another significant advantage for organizations. Freed from geographic constraints, employers can recruit highly specialized professionals from around the world, ensuring they secure the best skills and expertise. This diversity of thought and background often leads to more creative problem-solving and a stronger competitive edge. Additionally, remote work can improve employee retention rates: many workers cite flexibility and work-life balance as top priorities when choosing an employer, so offering remote options helps companies attract and keep top talent.

From an operational standpoint, remote work can boost productivity and efficiency. Studies have shown that employees working from home often experience fewer interruptions and can tailor their work environment to their needs, leading to higher focus and output. Time saved on commuting can be repurposed for work tasks or personal rejuvenation, reducing stress and burnout. Employers who adopt asynchronous communication and clear outcome-based performance metrics find that distributed teams can achieve—and sometimes exceed—their goals with less micromanagement.

Employees reap a host of personal and professional benefits from remote work as well. Foremost among these is flexibility: workers can design schedules that align with their peak productivity hours, caregiving responsibilities, or personal interests. Eliminating daily commutes not only saves time and money but also contributes to better mental health by reducing travel-related stress. Remote work often empowers individuals to live in locations with lower costs of living or closer to family, enhancing overall well-being and financial stability.

The autonomy inherent in remote roles fosters a sense of trust and accountability. As employees take ownership of their workflows and deliverables, they develop stronger self-management skills and professional confidence. Many also report improved work-life integration: by blending work and personal activities throughout the day—such as exercising during breaks or attending to family needs—individuals can maintain healthier routines and avoid the rigid boundaries of traditional office hours.

While remote work is not without its challenges, the benefits it delivers to both employers and employees are compelling. Organizations can operate more efficiently, access global talent, and reduce costs, while individuals enjoy greater flexibility, autonomy, and improved quality of life. Together, these advantages create a more resilient, engaged, and innovative workforce—one that is well-equipped to thrive in the evolving world of work.

Tools and Technologies Enabling Remote Work

A robust ecosystem of tools and technologies underpins today's remote work environments, enabling teams to collaborate seamlessly, maintain security, and manage projects across time zones. At the foundation are cloud-based productivity suites such as Google Workspace and Microsoft 365, which provide real-time co-editing of documents, spreadsheets, and presentations. These platforms synchronize changes instantly, allowing multiple contributors to work on a single file without version conflicts, and integrate with email, calendar, and file storage to centralize workflows.

Communication tools have become indispensable for replicating the immediacy of in-office interactions. Video conferencing applications like Zoom, Microsoft Teams, and Google Meet not only facilitate face-to-face meetings but also offer features such as screen sharing, virtual whiteboards, and breakout rooms for small-group discussions. Persistent chat platforms such as Slack and Discord complement these video tools by supporting topic-based channels, direct messaging, and searchable archives, so teams can maintain ongoing conversations without cluttering email inboxes.

Project management and task-tracking systems bring structure and accountability to distributed teams. Software like Asana, Trello, Jira, and Monday.com lets managers create boards or kanban workflows, assign tasks with due dates, and visualize progress through customizable dashboards. Automated notifications keep everyone informed when tasks change status, and integrations with version control systems (e.g., GitHub, GitLab) link code commits directly to project tickets, streamlining development cycles.

Secure remote access and network protection are critical for safeguarding corporate data. Virtual private networks (VPNs) encrypt traffic between home devices and company servers, while zero-trust network access (ZTNA) solutions—such as Cisco Duo or Zscaler—verify each user and device before granting entry to specific applications. Multi-factor authentication adds another layer of defense, requiring a second verification step via SMS, authenticator apps, or hardware tokens. Endpoint management platforms monitor and update remote devices to ensure compliance with security policies and deploy patches automatically.

File sharing and collaboration often rely on dedicated services like Dropbox, Box, or OneDrive, which synchronize folders across devices and provide granular permission controls. Teams can share large files securely without resorting to email attachments, and administrators can track access logs and enforce expiration dates on shared links. For design and creative work, cloud-based tools such as Figma and Adobe Creative Cloud allow teams to co-create graphics, wireframes, and prototypes, with version history and commenting built in.

To support brainstorming and planning, digital whiteboard apps like Miro and Mural offer infinite canvases where participants can place sticky notes, draw diagrams, and vote on ideas in real time. Time-tracking and productivity analytics tools—such as Toggl, Harvest, and RescueTime—help individuals and managers understand where hours are spent and identify opportunities for process improvements.

Together, these converging technologies have transformed remote work from a temporary workaround into a mature, resilient model. By integrating communication, collaboration, security, and project management into a cohesive digital workplace, organizations empower employees to stay connected, productive, and secure—no matter where they are located.

Chapter 3
Automation and AI in the Workforce

Automation and artificial intelligence (AI) are revolutionizing the workplace by taking on tasks that were once the sole domain of human workers. At its core, automation involves using machines or software to perform repetitive, rule-based processes with speed and precision. Early examples include assembly-line robots in manufacturing plants, programmed to weld car frames or package goods. Today, sophisticated AI systems extend automation into cognitive realms: algorithms can analyze vast datasets, recognize patterns, and make decisions without direct human oversight.

Industries across the board are experiencing AI-driven change. In manufacturing, collaborative robots—"cobots"—work alongside humans to boost efficiency and safety. In logistics, AI optimizes routes and inventory through real-time analytics, reducing costs and delivery times. The financial sector relies on AI for fraud detection and algorithmic trading, where machines execute trades in microseconds based on market signals. Healthcare providers employ AI to assist with diagnostic imaging, flagging potential issues for radiologists to review, while customer-service centers use chatbots to handle routine inquiries around the clock.

As automation and AI spread, they are not replacing humans wholesale but reshaping roles and responsibilities. Routine, predictable tasks are increasingly automated, freeing employees to focus on higher-value activities—creative problem-solving, strategic planning, and complex interpersonal interactions. This shift calls for new skill sets: workers must develop analytic thinking, digital literacy, and the ability to collaborate with AI tools. Training programs and lifelong learning initiatives are essential to help employees adapt and thrive.

Looking ahead, the future of human-AI collaboration promises a partnership where strengths are combined. Machines will handle data-heavy and repetitive tasks, while humans guide strategy, exercise empathy, and navigate ethical considerations. Organizations that embrace this synergy—investing in both technology and people—will unlock greater innovation and resilience. In this evolving landscape, the workplace becomes less about manual labor and more about harnessing intelligent systems to amplify human potential.

What is Automation and How Does It Work?

Automation refers to the use of technology—ranging from simple mechanical devices to advanced software and artificial intelligence—to perform tasks with minimal human intervention. At its simplest, automation replaces manual, repetitive actions with machines or programs that follow predefined rules. In manufacturing, this might involve conveyor belts and robotic arms that weld, paint, or assemble products. In the digital realm, it often takes the form of software "bots" or scripts that execute routine processes—such as data entry, invoice processing, or system monitoring—according to precise instructions.

At the heart of most automated systems lies a control mechanism that senses the current state of a process, compares it to a desired set of parameters, and then makes adjustments to maintain or correct performance. In industrial settings, sensors gather data on temperature, pressure, speed, or position. That data is fed into a controller—historically a programmable logic controller (PLC), and increasingly cloud-connected or AI-powered systems—which executes logic written by engineers. Based on that logic, actuators then drive motors, valves, or other hardware to achieve the intended outcome, such as slowing a conveyor belt or increasing coolant flow. This feedback loop, known as closed-loop control, ensures consistent quality and safety.

In software environments, automation often takes the form of workflow engines or robotic process automation (RPA). Workflow engines orchestrate a sequence of tasks—such as document approvals—by routing information between users and systems, enforcing deadlines and business rules. RPA tools, by contrast, mimic human interactions with software interfaces. They can log into applications, click through menus, extract data, and enter it elsewhere, all at machine speed. While traditional automation excels at rule-based, high-volume tasks, modern advancements integrate machine learning models that adapt to variations. An intelligent automation platform might analyze patterns in incoming emails, classify them, and decide autonomously which department should handle each request.

As automation evolves, the line between simple task execution and autonomous decision-making is blurring. Industrial robots are increasingly equipped with vision systems that allow them to recognize parts in different orientations and adjust on the fly. Software bots are becoming capable of handling exceptions—unexpected scenarios that fall outside standard rules—by consulting AI models trained on historical data. This convergence of robotics, AI, and cloud computing is creating systems that not only execute but also optimize processes continuously, identifying bottlenecks and suggesting improvements.

Ultimately, the power of automation lies in its ability to execute tasks faster, more accurately, and around the clock, freeing human workers to focus on creative problem-solving, strategic thinking, and interpersonal collaboration. By understanding how sensors, controllers, actuators, and software components interact in feedback loops, organizations can design reliable automated solutions that enhance productivity, quality, and safety across a wide range of industries.

Industries Most Affected by AI and Robotics

Advancements in artificial intelligence (AI) and robotics are reshaping industries across the global economy, driving efficiency gains, cost reductions, and new service paradigms. While virtually every sector will feel these effects, several industries stand out as particularly transformed.

1. Manufacturing

Manufacturing was among the first to embrace automation, with industrial robots handling repetitive tasks such as welding, painting, and assembly. Today's "smart factories" integrate AI-driven vision systems that enable robots to identify and manipulate parts with precision, even when presented in random orientations. Predictive maintenance platforms use AI to analyze sensor data from equipment, forecasting failures before they occur and minimizing downtime. These innovations boost throughput, improve product quality, and reduce labor costs.

2. Logistics and Supply Chain

AI and robotics are revolutionizing logistics by optimizing everything from warehouse operations to last-mile delivery. Automated guided vehicles (AGVs) and robotic pick-and-place systems sort and retrieve goods, working alongside human workers in dynamic environments. AI-powered route-planning algorithms analyze real-time traffic, weather, and delivery constraints to minimize transit times and fuel consumption. In fulfillment centers, machine learning models forecast demand patterns, enabling proactive inventory management and reducing stockouts.

3. Healthcare

In healthcare, AI algorithms assist in medical imaging by detecting anomalies in X-rays, MRIs, and CT scans more quickly and, in some cases, more accurately than human radiologists. Robotic surgical systems provide surgeons with enhanced dexterity and control for minimally invasive procedures. AI-driven diagnostic tools analyze patient records, lab results, and genetic data to recommend personalized treatment plans. Meanwhile, robotic process automation (RPA) streamlines administrative tasks such as patient scheduling, billing, and claims processing, reducing errors and freeing staff to focus on patient care.

4. Finance and Banking

The finance sector leverages AI for algorithmic trading, where machines execute high-frequency trades based on real-time market data and predictive models. Credit scoring models employ machine learning to assess borrower risk more comprehensively, considering nontraditional data sources such as social media and transaction histories. Chatbots and virtual assistants handle routine customer inquiries—balance checks, transaction histories, and simple account changes—24/7, improving service while cutting call-center volumes.

5. Retail and E-Commerce

Retailers use AI to personalize shopping experiences, recommending products based on browsing and purchase histories. Inventory robots in large warehouses scan shelves, identify low-stock items, and even reorder products automatically. At checkout, computer vision enables cashier-less stores, where customers simply pick up items and exit, with AI systems charging them automatically. These applications enhance customer convenience and streamline operations.

6. Agriculture

Agricultural robotics and AI are addressing labor shortages and sustainability challenges. Autonomous tractors plant and harvest crops with GPS precision. Drone-mounted sensors gather crop health data—moisture levels, nutrient deficiencies, pest infestations—which AI analyzes to generate optimized irrigation, fertilization, and pesticide plans. These practices increase yields while minimizing environmental impact.

Across these industries, the integration of AI and robotics is not about wholesale replacement of humans but about augmenting human capabilities. By automating routine and data-intensive tasks, these technologies enable workers to focus on complex problem-solving, creative design, and strategic decision-making—roles that remain distinctly human.

The Future of Human-AI Collaboration

The future of human-AI collaboration hinges on a symbiotic relationship in which each party leverages its unique strengths. As AI systems become more sophisticated, they will shoulder an increasing share of data-intensive, repetitive, and high-speed tasks. Human workers, in turn, will focus on strategic thinking, complex problem solving, and the emotional intelligence that machines cannot replicate. This division of labor will not only boost productivity but also enable more fulfilling and creative roles for people.

One emerging model is the "co-bot" or collaborative robot, which works side by side with humans on factory floors, in laboratories, and even in offices. Unlike traditional industrial robots that operate behind safety cages, co-bots are equipped with sensors and AI algorithms that allow them to adapt in real time to human movements and environmental changes. This capability makes them ideal for tasks requiring both precision and human judgment—for example, assisting surgeons during delicate procedures or handling variable parts on an assembly line.

In knowledge-work settings, AI will increasingly act as an intelligent assistant. Natural language processing (NLP) tools will draft reports, summarize long documents, and propose data-driven insights, all while learning a user's preferences and style. Augmented reality (AR) interfaces may overlay contextual information onto a user's workspace—highlighting relevant metrics during a video conference or suggesting design adjustments as an architect sketches. These AI-powered augmentations will accelerate decision-making and reduce cognitive load.

Ethical design principles and human oversight will be critical as collaboration deepens. Organizations must implement transparent AI systems that allow users to understand how recommendations are generated and to correct errors or biases. Training programs will need to equip workers not only with technical literacy—understanding model limitations, data provenance, and algorithmic fairness—but also with soft skills such as empathy, negotiation, and creative ideation that differentiate human contributions.

As AI takes on routine tasks, continuous learning will become central to career development. Employees will need to upskill in areas like data analysis, AI prompt engineering, and digital collaboration tools, while employers invest in mentorship and cross-functional teams that blend human and machine talents. New roles—such as AI ethicist, human-machine interface designer, and data curator—will emerge, reflecting the hybrid nature of future work.

Ultimately, the most successful human-AI partnerships will be those that respect the complementary capabilities of each. By combining AI's speed, scalability, and analytical power with human creativity, judgment, and emotional intelligence, organizations can unlock innovation at unprecedented scale. The future of work will not be humans versus machines but rather humans empowered by machines—together solving problems more effectively than either could alone.

Chapter 4
The Rise of the Gig Economy

The gig economy has emerged as a powerful force redefining how people work, earn, and build careers. What began as occasional freelance side projects has blossomed into a global marketplace where millions of individuals choose flexible, task-based opportunities over traditional employment. Advances in digital platforms and mobile technology have lowered barriers to entry, allowing workers with diverse skills—from graphic design and coding to ride-hailing and home repairs—to connect with clients and customers instantly. As companies seek agility and cost efficiency, they increasingly turn to gig workers to fill short-term needs, scaling their workforce up or down without the commitments of full-time hiring.

At the heart of this transformation are online marketplaces and apps that match supply with demand in real time. Platforms such as Upwork, Fiverr, and 99designs enable creative professionals to showcase portfolios and bid on projects, while services like Uber, Lyft, and DoorDash allow drivers and couriers to set their own schedules and earn on their own terms. Behind the scenes, sophisticated algorithms optimize job assignments, prices, and worker ratings, creating a dynamic ecosystem that responds instantly to market conditions. These technologies empower workers to access global opportunities that would have been unimaginable just a decade ago.

Yet the gig economy is a double-edged sword. On one hand, it offers unprecedented flexibility, autonomy, and the potential for higher earnings, particularly for those who can manage multiple gigs or carve out specialized niches. Gig work can provide income streams for students, parents, retirees, and anyone seeking supplemental earnings. On the other hand, many gig roles lack the stability, benefits, and legal protections associated with traditional employment. Gig workers often navigate unpredictable income, limited social safety nets, and classification debates over whether they are independent contractors or employees entitled to labor safeguards. These challenges raise important questions about fairness, worker rights, and the societal responsibilities of platforms and policymakers alike as the gig economy continues to expand.

The Growth of Freelancing and Contract Work

The past decade has witnessed an unprecedented surge in freelancing and contract work, driven by technological advances, shifting corporate strategies, and changing worker preferences. The proliferation of high-speed internet, cloud-based collaboration tools, and mobile connectivity has made it possible for skilled professionals to offer their services from virtually anywhere. Designers, developers, writers, consultants, and virtually every type of knowledge worker can now tap into global marketplaces to find projects that match their expertise and interests, breaking free from the geographic and organizational constraints of traditional employment.

At the same time, businesses—large and small—have embraced a more flexible workforce model to remain agile and cost-effective. Hiring full-time staff for every specialized need can be expensive and slow; by engaging freelancers and independent contractors, companies can scale their teams up or down in response to project demands without incurring long-term obligations. This approach has been further fueled by talent shortages in critical fields like software engineering, data analytics, and digital marketing, prompting organizations to seek specialized skills through contract arrangements rather than extended recruitment cycles.

Marketplaces such as Upwork, Fiverr, Toptal, and Guru have played a pivotal role in formalizing and democratizing access to freelance opportunities. These platforms offer end-to-end solutions—including talent matching algorithms, reputation systems, secure payment processing, and dispute resolution—lowering barriers to entry for both newcomers and seasoned professionals. Workers build portfolios, earn ratings, and cultivate repeat clients, while businesses benefit from transparent pricing and vetted expertise. As user bases grow, these networks generate network effects, drawing more clients and talent into a self-reinforcing cycle of opportunity.

Demographically, the rise in freelancing reflects broader workforce trends. Millennials and Gen Z, in particular, prioritize autonomy, meaningful work, and work-life balance. Many choose contract roles to pursue passion projects, maintain multiple income streams, or accommodate caregiving and lifestyle preferences. At the same time, experienced professionals nearing retirement are turning to consulting and contract work to stay engaged without the demands of full-time roles. This diversity in the freelancer population enriches the talent pool, offering businesses access to a wider range of perspectives and experiences.

Despite its growth, the freelance economy faces challenges around income stability, benefits, and legal classification. Many freelancers experience feast-and-famine cycles, managing unpredictable cash flow and shouldering the burden of health insurance, retirement savings, and tax compliance. Governments and industry groups are exploring policy reforms—such as portable benefits and clearer contractor definitions—to address these gaps. Nevertheless, the momentum behind freelancing shows no sign of slowing. As digital platforms continue to evolve and corporate attitudes toward flexible work solidify, freelancing and contract work will remain integral to the modern labor market, reshaping how talent and opportunity connect in the years to come.

Platforms Empowering the Gig Economy

Digital platforms have been the backbone of the modern gig economy, connecting millions of independent workers with businesses and customers around the world. Marketplaces such as Upwork, Fiverr, and Toptal cater to knowledge-based freelancers— graphic designers, software developers, writers, and consultants— by providing robust talent-matching algorithms, secure payment systems, and reputation frameworks that build trust. Upwork's skill-based filters and time-tracking tools help clients monitor progress, while Fiverr's gig packages allow sellers to present clear service bundles and buyers to compare offerings at a glance. Toptal, by contrast, focuses on highly vetted talent, offering businesses rapid access to the top 3 percent of freelancers, which reduces hiring risk and accelerates project kick-off.

On-demand service platforms such as Uber, Lyft, and DoorDash have revolutionized transportation and delivery sectors. Drivers use mobile apps to find nearby ride requests or delivery orders, with built-in navigation, earnings dashboards, and passenger ratings ensuring transparency and accountability. Airbnb reimagined hospitality by allowing homeowners to list spare rooms or entire properties, turning underutilized real estate into income streams. Its integrated calendar management and secure payment processing enable hosts to set dynamic pricing and maintain high occupancy rates, while guests benefit from detailed reviews and standardized booking procedures.

TaskRabbit and Handy tackle local, task-based work—from furniture assembly and home repairs to cleaning and yard maintenance—by matching vetted service providers with homeowners in need. These platforms handle background checks, liability insurance, and payment, reducing friction for both parties. Professionals can set their own hourly rates, choose assignments that fit their schedules, and build long-term relationships with repeat clients through consistent ratings and reviews.

Creative and specialized marketplaces have also emerged. 99designs enables businesses to host design contests, crowd-sourcing dozens of concepts before selecting a favorite, while PlateIQ connects restaurants with freelance bookkeepers and accountants who understand the intricacies of invoicing and inventory. Even healthcare has its gig platforms—Nomad Health and CareLinx allow nurses, therapists, and caregivers to find short-term assignments in hospitals or private homes, managing credentials, compliance, and shift schedules through intuitive dashboards.

Behind all these platforms lie powerful data-driven features: dynamic pricing models adjust rates in response to demand; recommendation engines suggest optimal gigs for workers based on past performance; and predictive analytics help businesses forecast staffing needs and budget accordingly. Mobile-first interfaces ensure that workers literally carry their virtual workplaces in their pockets, receiving push notifications for new opportunities and updating availability in real time. By automating onboarding, payment, and quality control, these platforms empower individuals to monetize their skills and assets with unprecedented ease, while enabling businesses to scale flexibly and tap into global talent pools on demand.

The Pros and Cons of Gig Work

Gig work offers unparalleled flexibility, allowing individuals to choose projects that align with their skills, interests, and schedules. Workers can accept assignments on their own terms, deciding when and where to work without the constraints of fixed office hours. This autonomy often leads to increased job satisfaction, as people balance professional commitments with personal priorities—whether that means caring for family members, pursuing education, or traveling. Earnings potential can also rise for those who cultivate specialized niches or maintain strong client relationships, since top-rated freelancers and drivers can command premium rates or surge pricing.

Access to a global marketplace is another advantage. Through digital platforms, gig workers tap into demand across industries and geographies, rather than being limited by local job markets. A graphic designer in Karachi can land clients in New York; a software developer in Nairobi can contribute to teams in Berlin. This borderless opportunity fosters diversity and inclusion, as talent from underrepresented regions competes on equal footing. Furthermore, gig work serves as an entry point for segments of the population who face barriers to traditional employment—students, retirees, and those with disabilities can generate income while leveraging their unique capabilities.

Despite these merits, gig work presents significant challenges. Income volatility ranks highest among them: unpredictable demand can lead to feast-and-famine cycles, making budgeting difficult. Without guaranteed hours or ongoing contracts, workers frequently face gaps between assignments and may struggle to cover fixed expenses during slow periods. Unlike salaried positions, gig roles rarely include benefits such as health insurance, paid leave, or retirement contributions, pushing individuals to secure and fund these protections independently—often at higher cost.

Legal and regulatory ambiguity further complicates gig work. Classification disputes over whether workers are independent contractors or employees have erupted worldwide, affecting access to labor rights and social safety nets. Platforms may shift policies or fee structures with little warning, altering take-home pay overnight. Workers also bear responsibility for taxes, licensing, and business expenses—expenses that traditional employers typically absorb. High platform fees can further erode earnings, especially for those operating on thin margins.

Isolation and lack of community pose additional downsides. Without a physical workplace or consistent teammates, gig workers may miss out on mentorship, collaboration, and social interaction. Developing soft skills like teamwork and navigating office politics can be more difficult, potentially hindering long-term career growth. Mental health can suffer when work and life boundaries blur, and feelings of disconnect grow.

In sum, gig work's freedom and opportunity come at the cost of stability and protection. Success requires self-discipline, financial planning, and proactive skills development. For those who thrive on autonomy and can manage the risks, gig roles offer a rewarding alternative to traditional employment—but not without trade-offs that demand careful consideration.

Chapter 5
The Digital Nomad Lifestyle

The Digital Nomad Lifestyle represents a radical departure from conventional work arrangements, allowing individuals to blend professional pursuits with exploration of the world. Fueled by high-speed internet, affordable travel, and a growing acceptance of remote roles, location-independent careers have surged in popularity. Writers draft manuscripts from beachside cafés, designers collaborate with clients while island-hopping, and developers code from mountain retreats—demonstrating that work need no longer be tied to a single physical place.

Balancing work and travel requires intentional planning and adaptability. Digital nomads often structure their days around time zones, aligning key meetings with clients or teams spread across continents. They carve out dedicated "office hours" wherever they settle—whether that's a co-working space in Bali, a rented apartment in Lisbon, or a hostel bunk in Chiang Mai—and embrace routines that foster productivity amid constantly changing surroundings. At the same time, they build in flexibility, using weekends or slow workdays to explore new cities, learn local languages, or pursue outdoor adventures.

The lifestyle also demands strong self-management skills. Without the cues of a traditional office—colleagues stopping by a desk or a daily commute—nomads must maintain discipline, set clear goals, and avoid distractions. They prioritize reliable internet access above all else, often scouting accommodations or co-working hubs based on network speed, power reliability, and community vibe. Budgeting becomes an exercise in precision, as costs for visas, travel, and lodging can fluctuate dramatically between regions.

Fortunately, a rich ecosystem of tools and technologies supports this way of life. Cloud storage and collaboration platforms keep files accessible from anywhere, while video-conferencing apps enable face-to-face conversations across thousands of miles. Project management tools help track deadlines, and time-zone converters prevent meeting mishaps. Niche apps exist for everything from finding last-minute accommodation deals to local SIM-card purchasing and global health-insurance coverage. Social networks and online communities connect nomads around the globe, offering advice on the best coworking spots, visa requirements, and cultural etiquette.

Ultimately, the Digital Nomad Lifestyle is about freedom, adaptability, and the courage to pursue work on one's own terms. It requires balancing the thrill of discovery with the discipline of remote work, but for those who master both, the world becomes not just a destination but an extension of the office.

The Rise of Location-Independent Careers

The concept of earning a living without being tethered to a single location has moved from a fringe phenomenon to a mainstream career choice. Advances in broadband connectivity and cloud-based services have made it possible for professionals in fields such as software development, design, writing, marketing, and consulting to perform their roles from virtually anywhere. Companies that once required staff to be physically present have increasingly shifted toward flexible policies, recognizing that productivity is tied more to deliverables than to desk time. This evolution has been accelerated by global events and cultural shifts that emphasize work-life balance, autonomy, and the pursuit of personal passions alongside professional goals.

Demographic and economic trends have also played a key role. Millennials and members of Generation Z prioritize experiences and personal growth, often valuing travel and cultural immersion as much as—or more than—traditional markers of success. Meanwhile, rising costs of urban living in technology hubs have encouraged many to decouple income from place, opting instead for regions with lower overhead while maintaining access to high-paying clients or employers. Employers, for their part, have realized that remote talent pools offer access to specialized skills without the constraints of local labor markets, enabling them to assemble diverse, global teams that bring varied perspectives to problem-solving.

Institutional support structures have emerged to facilitate this shift. Co-working spaces now dot major cities and small towns alike, providing reliable internet, meeting rooms, and a sense of community for location-independent professionals. Online platforms offer not only job listings but also resources for setting up entities abroad, managing international tax obligations, and securing health insurance across borders. Digital nomad visas and remote-worker permits have been introduced by countries seeking to attract long-term visitors who contribute to local economies through lodging, dining, and entertainment.

Educational offerings have adapted as well. Universities and training providers now offer certificates and degrees in areas such as data analytics, UX/UI design, and digital marketing—fields particularly well-suited to remote work. Webinars and virtual conferences allow professionals to network, share best practices, and stay current on industry trends without the need to travel. Mentorship programs and online communities provide peer support, addressing challenges of isolation and skill development in a dispersed workforce.

As location-independent careers grow, they are reshaping conventional notions of employment. Workers no longer view their careers as tied to a particular employer or office; instead, many curate portfolios of projects and clients, building personal brands that transcend geographic boundaries. This shift empowers individuals to explore new cultures, maintain healthier work-life integration, and respond more nimbly to market changes. At the same time, it challenges organizations and policymakers to rethink labor regulations, social safety nets, and community infrastructures, ensuring that the benefits of this transformation extend equitably across the global workforce.

Managing Work and Travel Simultaneously

Balancing work and travel requires intentional planning, disciplined routines, and the ability to adapt to changing circumstances. The first step is establishing a reliable workspace wherever you go. Before booking accommodations, research internet speeds and connectivity options: read reviews on sites like Nomad

List or check if local cafés and coworking spaces offer day passes. Investing in a portable Wi-Fi hotspot or an international data plan can provide a crucial backup when hotel connections falter.

Time management is key. Begin each week by mapping out your commitments alongside your travel itinerary. Use calendar tools that display multiple time zones—such as World Time Buddy or the built-in features of Google Calendar—to schedule meetings without confusion. Block "focus hours" each day during your peak productivity window, and communicate these clearly to colleagues and clients so they know when you're available. Protect these blocks by turning off notifications and setting a simple status message in chat tools that you're in "deep work" mode.

Maintaining routines helps ground you amid constant movement. Even if your workday looks different from one location to the next, carve out rituals: a morning stretch or brief meditation, a consistent breakfast, or a walk to a favorite local café. These small anchors can boost focus and signal to your brain that it's time to switch into work mode. Likewise, establish a clear cutoff at the end of your workday, whether it's closing your laptop by 6 p.m. or taking a brief walk to transition into leisure. This boundary prevents work from bleeding into your travel experiences and helps combat burnout.

Efficient packing and gear selection also streamline the process. Limit luggage to essential tech—a lightweight laptop, noise-canceling headphones, and a compact power strip—and carry requisite adapters for each country. Use packing cubes to organize chargers, cables, and accessories so you can set up your workspace quickly upon arrival.

Finally, leverage local environments for both productivity and inspiration. Schedule shorter work sessions during the hottest part of the day, then explore sites or local events in the afternoon. Many nomads adopt a "work in the morning, play in the afternoon" rhythm that aligns with both energy levels and daylight hours. If deadlines demand longer stretches, reward yourself with a sunset hike or an evening cultural activity once tasks are complete.

By combining proactive logistics—like vetting Wi-Fi options and mastering time-zone tools—with personal routines and mindful boundaries, you can thrive as a digital nomad. Managing work alongside travel becomes not just a challenge to endure but an opportunity to integrate professional goals with rich, on-the-ground experiences.

The Tools and Technologies for Digital Nomads

A robust suite of digital tools and technologies forms the backbone of any successful digital nomad's workflow, enabling seamless communication, reliable connectivity, efficient project management, and personal organization on the go.

Reliable internet access is paramount. Many nomads invest in portable Wi-Fi hotspots—such as Skyroam or GlocalMe—that provide cellular-backed broadband in dozens of countries. In regions with patchy coverage, a dual-SIM smartphone or an unlocked device paired with local prepaid data plans can serve as a dependable backup. Virtual private networks (VPNs) like ExpressVPN or NordVPN ensure secure connections on public Wi-Fi and help maintain privacy when accessing sensitive work resources.

Communication and collaboration platforms replicate the dynamics of a modern office. Video-conferencing tools like Zoom, Microsoft Teams, or Google Meet support high-definition calls and screen sharing, while persistent chat apps such as Slack or Discord organize conversations into topic-focused channels and direct messages. Cloud collaboration suites—Google Workspace or Microsoft 365—allow real-time co-editing of documents, spreadsheets, and presentations, eliminating version conflicts and centralizing email, calendar, and file storage.

Project management tools keep tasks and deadlines visible across dispersed teams. Trello's kanban boards, Asana's list and timeline views, and ClickUp's customizable workflows let nomads track assignments, assign responsibilities, and monitor progress through automated notifications. Time-zone converters like World Time Buddy or Every Time Zone help prevent scheduling mishaps by displaying multiple zones side by side, ensuring meetings align across continents.

File storage and sharing services—Dropbox, Box, or OneDrive—synchronize folders across all devices and support granular permission controls. Digital nomads can share large media files or project assets without clogging email, and administrators can enforce link expiration dates and track access logs for compliance. For design and creative work, cloud-based platforms like Figma or Adobe Creative Cloud permit collaborative wireframing, prototyping, and visual asset management with built-in commenting.

Personal productivity and well-being tools guard against burnout and time mismanagement. Time-tracking apps such as Toggl or RescueTime provide insights into where hours are spent, helping nomads identify distractions and optimize daily routines. Focus and mindfulness apps like Forest or Headspace support concentration and mental health, encouraging regular breaks and stress relief.

Travel logistics are simplified through aggregators like Skyscanner and Google Flights for cheap airfare, and accommodation platforms—Airbnb, Booking.com, or digital-nomad-focused services like Nomad List—surface vetted co-working spaces, reliable internet cafés, and community hubs. Finance and payment apps—Wise (formerly TransferWise), Revolut, or PayPal—enable low-cost cross-border transfers, multi-currency accounts, and receipt scanning, helping nomads manage budgets and invoice clients globally.

Security and password management—via tools like 1Password or LastPass—protect credentials across multiple accounts, while portable hardware essentials (lightweight laptops, noise-canceling headphones, compact power strips, and external SSDs) ensure digital nomads can set up ergonomic workstations almost anywhere.

Together, these interconnected tools empower digital nomads to stay productive, secure, and organized, turning any corner of the world into an efficient, fully functional office.

Chapter 6
Reskilling and Up-skilling for the Future

In an era defined by rapid technological change and shifting economic landscapes, the ability to learn, adapt, and grow has become more than an advantage—it is a necessity. As automation and artificial intelligence reconfigure industries, roles that once relied on routine tasks are disappearing or evolving, while entirely new career paths emerge. Lifelong learning ensures that individuals remain relevant and employable, able to pivot in response to market demands rather than being left behind. Embracing a mindset of continuous development not only safeguards against redundancy but also opens doors to higher-value work and personal fulfillment.

The skills demanded by tomorrow's job market often extend far beyond technical expertise. Critical thinking and complex problem-solving will be prized as organizations seek employees who can interpret data insights, navigate uncertainty, and craft innovative solutions. Digital literacy—including comfort with cloud platforms, basic coding, and data visualization—serves as a baseline for virtually any role. Equally important are interpersonal abilities such as creativity, emotional intelligence, and cross-cultural communication, which machines cannot replicate and which foster effective collaboration in diverse, distributed teams. Mastering these competencies empowers workers to contribute meaningfully, regardless of industry.

Finding the right learning opportunities can feel daunting amid the vast array of options. Traditional avenues such as university degrees and professional certificates coexist with online courses, micro-credentials, and industry boot camps. Mentorship programs, peer learning communities, and on-the-job training offer practical experience alongside theoretical knowledge. The key is to align growth paths with personal goals and market needs—conducting regular skills audits, seeking feedback, and staying attuned to emerging trends. A portfolio approach, in which learners document completed projects and certifications, helps demonstrate competence to prospective employers or clients.

Ultimately, reskilling and up-skilling are not one-off efforts but ongoing commitments. By treating learning as a continual journey rather than a finite milestone, individuals can navigate career transitions with confidence and agility. Organizations that support these endeavors—through funding, time allowances, and culture—benefit from a more engaged, innovative workforce. In this dynamic landscape, those who cultivate a habit of learning will not only survive but thrive, shaping the future rather than merely reacting to it.

Why Lifelong Learning is Essential

In today's rapidly evolving economy, the concept of finishing formal education and then coasting on existing skills is no longer viable. Technological advances—from automation and artificial intelligence to blockchain and biotechnology—continually redefine job requirements and render once-sought expertise obsolete. Lifelong learning provides the means to stay current, ensuring that individuals can adapt as roles change, industries shift, and new opportunities emerge. Rather than waiting for a crisis or layoff to prompt upskilling, continuous learning enables proactive career management, reducing the risk of redundancy and maintaining professional relevance.

Beyond safeguarding against obsolescence, lifelong learning fuels personal growth and job satisfaction. Engaging with new subjects or techniques broadens perspectives, rekindles curiosity, and combats stagnation. Workers who pursue ongoing development often report greater confidence, motivation, and a stronger sense of purpose—factors linked to higher performance and lower burnout. Additionally, the process of acquiring new knowledge and mastering fresh challenges reinforces cognitive flexibility, sharpening problem-solving abilities that are critical in dynamic work environments.

Organizations also benefit when employees embrace a learning mindset. Companies that support reskilling and upskilling initiatives foster cultures of innovation and resilience. When teams view change as an opportunity rather than a threat, they become more agile in responding to market disruptions, experimenting with new approaches, and implementing cutting-edge solutions. Investing in employee development enhances retention, as individuals feel valued and see clear pathways for advancement. In turn, businesses secure the talent necessary to compete and grow in an ever-shifting landscape.

Lifelong learning need not be confined to traditional academic routes. Individuals can choose from a diverse mix of formal and informal options: online courses, micro-credentials, industry certifications, workshops, webinars, mentorships, and peer-led study groups. Many platforms offer modular, self-paced curricula that fit around full-time work, making it easier to integrate development into daily routines. The key is to identify emerging trends—such as data literacy, digital marketing, or ethical AI—and target learning efforts accordingly, using short-term goals and regular reflection to track progress. By documenting achievements in a personal portfolio or professional network, learners create tangible proof of their evolving skill set.

Ultimately, lifelong learning transforms career trajectories from linear paths into dynamic journeys of continuous growth. It empowers individuals to anticipate change, seize new roles, and contribute meaningfully to their organizations and communities. In a world where adaptability is the ultimate differentiator, those who embrace perpetual learning will not only thrive professionally but also shape the future of work itself.

Key Skills for the Future Job Market

As the nature of work evolves, certain competencies will become increasingly valuable across industries. Foremost among these is complex problem-solving: the ability to define multifaceted challenges, evaluate diverse data sources, and devise innovative solutions. As routine tasks are automated, employees who can navigate ambiguity, synthesize information, and apply critical thinking will stand out. This skill requires both analytical rigor and creative insight, enabling individuals to tackle novel situations rather than rely on practiced routines.

Digital literacy represents another cornerstone for future employability. Comfort with cloud-based tools, collaboration platforms, and basic coding concepts allows workers to engage fully in technology-driven environments. Beyond knowing how to click through software interfaces, digitally literate professionals understand data structures, privacy considerations, and the potential of emerging technologies. They can automate simple workflows, interpret analytics dashboards, and collaborate effectively with technical teams, serving as bridges between business needs and technical execution.

Emotional intelligence—the capacity to perceive, understand, and manage one's own emotions and those of others—will remain a uniquely human strength in an increasingly automated world. As organizations become more virtual and distributed, the ability to build trust, resolve conflicts, and foster inclusive teamwork takes on added importance. Leaders and contributors who listen actively, demonstrate empathy, and adapt communication styles will create stronger bonds and higher engagement among colleagues, even when face-to-face contact is limited.

Adaptability and learning agility are also essential, as workers must continually update their skill sets to keep pace with technological change. Those who embrace growth mindsets— viewing challenges as opportunities to learn rather than threats— will more readily pivot between roles, acquire new competencies, and thrive in dynamic work environments. Continuous learning habits, such as setting regular learning goals, seeking feedback, and experimenting with new tools, ensure that professionals remain relevant and resilient in the face of disruption.

Interdisciplinary collaboration underscores the value of blending expertise across domains. Complex projects often call for teams that combine technical, creative, and operational perspectives. Individuals who can translate jargon between specialists, integrate diverse viewpoints, and co-design solutions with cross-functional colleagues will accelerate innovation and drive holistic outcomes. This requires both domain knowledge and strong communication skills to bridge gaps and align objectives.

Finally, ethical judgment and systems thinking will rise in prominence as technology's impact deepens. Understanding the broader consequences of design choices—whether in algorithmic bias, environmental sustainability, or social equity—enables workers to advocate for responsible practices and long-term value creation. Systems thinkers see how individual tasks fit into larger organizational and societal frameworks, helping prevent unintended harm and ensuring that progress benefits stakeholders equitably.

Together, these skills form a foundation for success in the future job market. By cultivating problem-solving prowess, digital fluency, emotional intelligence, adaptability, interdisciplinary collaboration, and ethical judgment, individuals position themselves not only to survive but to lead in a rapidly changing world.

How to Find the Right Learning Opportunities

Finding the right learning opportunities begins with a clear understanding of your career goals and the skills you need to achieve them. Start by conducting a skills audit: list your current competencies alongside those required for your target roles. Compare this inventory with job postings, industry reports, and conversations with mentors or peers to identify gaps. This process not only highlights areas for development but also ensures that the time and resources you invest align directly with market demand and personal ambitions.

Once you have defined your learning objectives, explore a mix of formal and informal educational channels. Traditional institutions—universities, community colleges, and professional certification bodies—offer structured programs that carry recognized credentials. These can be particularly valuable in fields where accreditation matters, such as project management, cybersecurity, or accounting. Online course platforms like Coursera, edX, and Udacity provide modular, self-paced courses and "nanodegrees" in emerging areas like data science, machine learning, and digital marketing. Many partner with industry leaders, ensuring that course content reflects real-world practices and tools.

Equally important are hands-on experiences that bridge theory and practice. Boot camps, hackathons, and coding challenges immerse you in intensive, project-based learning, often under the guidance of seasoned practitioners. Internships or short-term consulting assignments—whether through gig platforms or company-sponsored apprenticeships—allow you to apply new skills in professional contexts and receive immediate feedback. Volunteering your expertise for non-profits or open-source projects can also expand your portfolio while demonstrating social impact.

To refine your choices, leverage trusted reviews and peer recommendations. Platforms such as LinkedIn Learning, Skillshare, and specialized forums often include ratings, learner testimonials, and instructor profiles that help you assess course quality. Join industry-specific communities—on Slack, Discord, or Reddit—to ask for firsthand experiences and compare different providers. Reach out to alumni or colleagues who have completed programs you're considering; their insights into curriculum relevance, pacing, and post-course support can guide your decision.

Budget and time constraints also factor into the selection process. Free or low-cost MOOCs and micro-courses can introduce new concepts without significant investment, allowing you to "test drive" topics before committing to longer programs. Meanwhile, employers may offer tuition reimbursement or allocate professional development budgets; inquire about internal training platforms and mentorship schemes. When evaluating paid options, review refund policies, scholarship opportunities, and payment plans to mitigate financial risk.

Finally, adopt a growth-oriented mindset by setting measurable milestones and seeking accountability. Create a personalized learning roadmap with timelines for completing modules, earning certifications, or delivering capstone projects. Share your goals with mentors or learning partners who can offer regular check-ins and constructive feedback. By aligning your ambitions with targeted resources, verifying quality through community insights, and maintaining disciplined progress tracking, you'll ensure that each learning opportunity advances your career and keeps you at the forefront of industry trends.

Chapter 7
Technology Shaping the Future of Work

Advances in technology are driving a fundamental transformation in the world of work, reshaping roles, processes, and organizational structures across every industry. At the forefront is artificial intelligence (AI), which harnesses vast amounts of data to automate complex tasks, generate insights, and augment human decision-making. From predictive analytics that optimize supply chains to intelligent assistants that draft emails or analyze legal contracts, AI is extending the reach of what machines can accomplish and forcing us to rethink the boundaries between routine and creative work.

Alongside AI, blockchain is emerging as a potential game-changer for employment and collaboration. By offering decentralized, tamper-proof ledgers, blockchain can streamline credential verification, ensuring that skills and qualifications are authentic and instantly verifiable. Smart contracts can automate payment and compliance for freelance or gig engagements, reducing administrative friction and fostering trust among parties who have never met. This technology may also enable new forms of decentralized organizations, where stakeholders govern themselves through transparent protocols rather than traditional hierarchies.

Automation, in its many forms, is another critical force redefining job roles. Robots and software bots are taking on repetitive, high-volume tasks—from data entry and assembly-line work to call-center inquiries—freeing human workers to focus on problem solving, innovation, and interpersonal collaboration. As automation becomes more sophisticated, it will not only replace manual tasks but also create entirely new categories of work: roles in robot maintenance, AI ethics, data curation, and human-machine interface design. The challenge will be to manage this transition so that displaced workers can reskill and step into emerging positions.

Taken together, these technologies are not merely incremental improvements but catalysts for a broader reimagining of work itself. Organizations that embrace AI, blockchain, and advanced automation stand to gain agility, efficiency, and competitive advantage. Workers who develop the skills to partner with and oversee these systems will find themselves in high demand. As the boundary between technology and labor blurs, the future of work will hinge on our ability to integrate human ingenuity with machine capability in ways that are both productive and equitable.

The Impact of Artificial Intelligence

Artificial intelligence (AI) is reshaping nearly every aspect of modern business and society, driving efficiency, innovation, and new forms of value creation. One of the most visible effects has been the automation of routine cognitive tasks. Algorithms now process invoices, sort emails, and analyze large datasets far more quickly and accurately than humans could, freeing workers to focus on strategic and creative activities. In customer service, chatbots and virtual assistants handle common inquiries around the clock, reducing wait times and allowing human agents to tackle complex or sensitive cases. In finance, AI models detect fraudulent transactions in real time, flagging suspicious activity before significant losses occur.

Beyond routine automation, AI's predictive power is transforming decision-making. In supply chain management, machine-learning models forecast demand fluctuations based on historical sales, weather patterns, and social media trends, enabling companies to optimize inventory, reduce waste, and improve customer satisfaction. Healthcare providers use AI to analyze medical images, identifying anomalies such as tumors or fractures with a level of consistency that rivals expert radiologists. These systems can triage urgent cases more rapidly, allowing clinicians to intervene earlier and improve patient outcomes.

At the same time, AI presents challenges related to workforce displacement and equity. As machines assume tasks once performed by humans, some roles—particularly those involving repetitive analysis or data entry—are at risk of obsolescence. Workers whose jobs are automated may struggle to find new employment without reskilling. However, AI also creates new opportunities: demand is rising for data scientists, AI ethics specialists, and roles in model governance, maintenance, and interpretation. Organizations that invest in training programs to help employees transition into these emerging roles can mitigate displacement risks and build more resilient talent pipelines.

Ethical considerations have come to the forefront as AI systems influence high-stakes decisions. Biases in training data can lead to unfair outcomes in hiring tools, lending decisions, or criminal justice assessments. Transparency and accountability frameworks are essential to ensure that AI recommendations are explainable and that humans remain in control of final choices. Regulators and industry groups are collaborating to develop guidelines that balance innovation with safeguards against misuse and discrimination.

Looking ahead, AI's greatest impact may lie in human–machine collaboration rather than wholesale automation. Augmented intelligence approaches prioritize systems that enhance human judgment, such as decision-support tools that surface relevant insights while leaving interpretation to professionals. In creative fields, AI can generate design prototypes or music compositions, serving as a catalyst for human creativity rather than a replacement. The organizations and workers who embrace AI as a partner—leveraging its strengths in data processing and pattern recognition while maintaining human empathy, ethics, and strategic vision—will be best positioned to thrive in the rapidly evolving world of work.

Blockchain and Its Potential in Employment

Blockchain technology, best known as the backbone of cryptocurrencies like Bitcoin and Ethereum, holds significant promise for reinventing traditional employment processes. At its core, blockchain is a distributed ledger that records transactions in immutable, time-stamped blocks shared across a network of computers. This decentralized structure eliminates the need for intermediaries—such as banks or clearinghouses—and ensures transparency, security, and tamper resistance, qualities that can address many inefficiencies in hiring, payroll, and workforce management.

One of the most immediate applications is credential verification. Onboarding new hires often involves background checks, degree authentication, and validation of professional licenses—a process that can take days or weeks. By storing academic credentials, certifications, and work histories on a blockchain, employers can instantly verify the authenticity of an applicant's qualifications. Institutions issue cryptographic "certificates" directly to the candidate's decentralized identity, and any employer can cross-reference these credentials against the ledger. This not only speeds up hiring but also reduces fraud.

Smart contracts—self-executing agreements encoded on a blockchain—can automate payroll and gig payments. Instead of processing timesheets, approvals, and manual disbursements, an organization could deploy a contract that releases funds automatically once predetermined conditions are met, such as project completion or approved hours logged. For gig workers, this ensures timely, trustless payment without the overhead of invoices or third-party payment processors. It also introduces programmable pay structures, such as micropayments for discrete tasks or tiered bonuses triggered by performance metrics.

Blockchain also enables new organizational models. Decentralized autonomous organizations (DAOs) operate through community-governed protocols rather than hierarchical management. Contributors earn tokens representing voting rights and economic stakes, aligning rewards with collective success. In such structures, roles and responsibilities emerge organically, and decision-making is transparent. Although still experimental, DAOs point to a future where employment is fluid and self-directed, with stakeholders collaborating on projects regardless of geographic or institutional boundaries.

Beyond hiring and payment, blockchain can enhance benefits administration and compliance. Companies can tokenize employee stock options, creating liquid digital assets that vest automatically according to predefined schedules. Audit trails for tax withholdings, insurance enrollment, and regulatory reporting become immutable records that simplify audits and reduce legal risk. Furthermore, blockchain's encryption and permission features protect sensitive personal data while granting employees selective control over who accesses their information.

Challenges remain—scalability issues, regulatory uncertainty, and integration with legacy systems—but pilot programs in human resources, freelancing marketplaces, and supply-chain firms demonstrate feasibility. As the technology matures, blockchain stands to transform employment by delivering speed, transparency, and flexibility, ushering in a more efficient and equitable world of work.

How Automation Will Redefine Jobs

As automation technologies become more sophisticated, they will fundamentally reshape the nature of jobs rather than simply eliminate roles outright. Routine, repetitive tasks—whether physical, such as assembly line welding, or cognitive, like invoice processing—are already being handled faster and more accurately by machines. Instead of viewing this as a zero-sum exchange, organizations are redesigning positions so that human workers focus on higher-value activities that demand creativity, critical thinking, and interpersonal skills. For example, rather than manually inspecting every product for defects, quality-control technicians now oversee intelligent vision systems, interpreting alerts and adapting inspection criteria to new production challenges.

As basic tasks are delegated to robots and software bots, new hybrid roles will emerge that blend technical oversight with domain expertise. Maintenance technicians will need to understand both mechanical systems and the data analytics platforms that predict equipment failures. Customer-service representatives will collaborate with AI-powered chatbots, stepping in only when emotional nuance or complex reasoning is required. These shifts will encourage lifelong learning, as workers refresh their skill sets to manage human-machine teams and integrate new tools into daily workflows.

Rather than simply eliminating jobs, automation will drive the creation of entirely new occupational categories. Designers of human-machine interfaces, specialists in algorithmic ethics, and data curators who ensure the integrity of training datasets will become essential. Some industries may see entire specialties emerge around monitoring, auditing, and improving automated systems. For instance, financial firms already employ "algorithm auditors" to validate trading models and guard against unintended biases or market manipulation.

At the same time, automation will redefine the organization of work itself. Traditional job descriptions, centered on a fixed set of tasks, will give way to project-based engagements and outcome-oriented roles. Workers will assemble into fluid teams that form around specific challenges—such as launching a new product or responding to a supply chain disruption—and then reconfigure as needs evolve. This fluidity will demand stronger collaboration tools, adaptable performance metrics, and a culture that values continuous experimentation over rigid hierarchy.

Geographic boundaries will also blur as remote management of automated operations becomes more common. Control centers could monitor fleets of autonomous vehicles or robotics-driven warehouses from anywhere in the world, supported by real-time analytics and cloud-based dashboards. This will open opportunities for talent in regions previously excluded from high-tech industries, while challenging local workforces to develop complementary skills.

Ultimately, automation will redefine jobs by elevating the roles that only humans can fulfill—those requiring empathy, strategic insight, and the ability to navigate uncertainty—while entrusting machines with precision, speed, and data-driven optimization. Workers and organizations that embrace this partnership, investing in training and redesigning roles around human-machine collaboration, will unlock greater innovation, resilience, and competitive advantage in the rapidly evolving world of work.

Chapter 8
Technology Shaping the Future of Work

Advancements in technology are not merely improving existing processes—they are redefining the very nature of work. Artificial intelligence, once confined to research labs, now powers decision-support systems that analyze vast datasets, predict trends, and automate routine tasks. Blockchain, originally designed for secure digital currencies, is finding applications in credential verification, transparent contract execution, and decentralized organizational models. Meanwhile, automation through robotics and software bots is transforming roles across industries, shifting human effort away from repetitive tasks and toward creative, strategic, and interpersonal functions.

As these technologies converge, the workplace becomes a dynamic ecosystem of humans and machines collaborating toward shared goals. AI-driven tools can handle data ingestion, pattern recognition, and basic problem-solving at machine speed, while humans provide context, ethical judgment, and innovation. Blockchain's immutable ledgers and smart contracts streamline administrative workflows—verifying credentials, automating payments, and enforcing agreements without intermediaries—

freeing workers to focus on complex value-creation activities. At the same time, automation reconfigures job designs: roles evolve into hybrid positions that oversee and optimize automated systems, blending technical oversight with domain expertise.

The impact of these shifts extends beyond individual tasks to organizational structures and employment models. Traditional hierarchies give way to fluid, project-based teams that form around specific challenges and disband when objectives are met. Geographic barriers dissolve as remote monitoring and management of automated operations become routine, opening global talent pools to firms of every size. Companies that embrace this technological triad—AI, blockchain, and automation—gain agility, reduce operational friction, and unlock new revenue streams. Workers who develop skills in human-machine collaboration, data stewardship, and ethical technology governance will find themselves in high demand.

Navigating this transformation requires more than technology adoption; it demands a cultural shift. Organizations must foster continuous learning, invest in upskilling, and embed ethical frameworks into technology design. As machines take on precision and scale, humans must redefine their contributions around creativity, empathy, and strategic vision. In this emerging landscape, the future of work will hinge on our ability to integrate technological prowess with human ingenuity, ensuring that progress benefits both businesses and the people who power them.

The Impact of Artificial Intelligence

Artificial intelligence (AI) has emerged as a transformative force across virtually every industry, driving dramatic improvements in efficiency, accuracy, and innovation. At its core, AI enables machines to perform tasks that once required significant human cognitive effort—such as pattern recognition, language comprehension, and decision-making—by leveraging large datasets and advanced algorithms. This capability not only accelerates routine processes but also uncovers insights buried within complex information, fundamentally reshaping how organizations operate.

One of the most visible impacts of AI is in data analysis. Businesses now employ machine-learning models to sift through massive volumes of customer behavior, financial transactions, or supply-chain metrics, identifying trends and anomalies far more quickly than traditional analytics tools. In retail, these insights allow for dynamic pricing and personalized marketing campaigns that adjust in real time to consumer preferences. In healthcare, AI-powered image analysis pinpoints potential health issues—such as early-stage tumors or retinal damage—in medical scans, assisting clinicians in making more accurate diagnoses and improving patient outcomes.

Automation of repetitive, manual tasks is another significant benefit. Chatbots and virtual assistants manage routine customer inquiries around the clock, reducing response times and freeing human agents to handle more nuanced or emotionally sensitive issues. In corporate settings, "robotic process automation" (RPA) bots execute transactional workflows—processing invoices, reconciling accounts, or generating reports—without fatigue or error. This shift not only lowers operational costs but also redeploys human talent to higher-value activities like strategic planning and creative problem-solving.

However, AI's rise brings challenges related to job displacement and skill requirements. As machines assume tasks formerly performed by humans, certain roles—particularly those centered on data entry, basic analysis, or simple pattern matching—face the risk of obsolescence. To address this, organizations must invest in reskilling and upskilling initiatives, preparing employees for new roles that involve overseeing AI systems, interpreting their outputs, and ensuring ethical use. Emerging occupations include AI ethicists, data curators, and human–machine interaction designers, all of which underscore the evolving collaboration between human insight and machine capability.

Ethical considerations are also paramount as AI systems influence critical decisions in hiring, lending, and legal contexts. Biases present in training data can perpetuate unfair outcomes, making transparency and accountability essential. Explainable AI techniques, which provide clear rationales for algorithmic choices, help build trust and enable oversight. Regulatory bodies and industry coalitions are increasingly advocating for standards that balance innovation with safeguards against misuse.

Looking forward, AI's most profound impact may lie in its ability to augment human creativity and strategic vision. By handling data-intensive tasks and providing predictive insights, AI becomes a collaborator—freeing individuals to focus on innovation, relationship-building, and complex ethical judgment. Organizations that integrate AI thoughtfully—blending technological prowess with human empathy and oversight—will unlock the greatest value, forging a future where machines amplify human potential rather than replace it.

Blockchain and Its Potential in Employment

Blockchain technology offers transformative potential for employment by introducing secure, transparent, and efficient ways to manage credentials, contracts, and workforce participation. At its core, a blockchain is a decentralized ledger maintained by a network of computers, where each transaction is time-stamped and immutable. This architecture removes the need for intermediaries—such as third-party verifiers or payroll processors—streamlining many administrative tasks in human resources.

One of the most immediate applications is credential verification. Traditionally, employers must manually authenticate degrees, certifications, and work histories, a process that can take days or weeks. By issuing educational credentials and professional licenses as cryptographically signed blockchain entries, institutions enable instant validation. A hiring manager can simply query the public ledger to confirm an applicant's qualifications without contacting multiple bodies, reducing fraud and administrative overhead.

Smart contracts further extend blockchain's value in employment. These are self-executing agreements encoded on the blockchain that automatically release payments or trigger actions once preset conditions are met. For freelance or gig workers, smart contracts can ensure immediate payment upon project completion, eliminating delays common with traditional invoicing. Employers benefit from reduced processing costs and improved cash flow forecasting, while workers gain trust in timely compensation.

Beyond individual transactions, blockchain enables entirely new organizational structures. Decentralized Autonomous Organizations (DAOs) operate through consensus mechanisms rather than hierarchical management. Contributors earn governance tokens that grant voting rights proportionate to their participation or investment. Decisions around project funding, resource allocation, and strategic direction are made collectively and transparently, aligning incentives and fostering community ownership. Though still nascent, DAOs hint at a future where employment is more fluid, with roles defined by contributions to shared goals rather than fixed job descriptions.

Moreover, blockchain can revolutionize benefits administration and equity compensation. Employee stock options can be tokenized, creating digital assets that vest on predetermined schedules and can be traded freely, increasing liquidity for employees. Benefit enrollments, such as health insurance or retirement plans, can be recorded on-chain, creating an auditable trail that simplifies compliance and audits. Workers maintain control over their personal data through private keys, sharing only the information necessary for each transaction and preserving privacy.

Challenges remain—including scalability, regulatory uncertainty, and integration with legacy systems—but pilot projects in HR tech and freelancing platforms demonstrate tangible benefits. As blockchain ecosystems mature, organizations that adopt these decentralized solutions stand to gain faster onboarding, reduced administrative costs, and innovative engagement models that empower workers. In doing so, they lay the groundwork for a more transparent, efficient, and equitable future of employment.

How Automation Will Redefine Jobs

As automation technologies advance, they will transform jobs by shifting the balance of responsibilities between humans and machines rather than simply eliminating roles. Routine, repetitive tasks—whether on an assembly line, in data entry, or in basic customer interactions—are increasingly performed by robots and software bots with greater speed and precision than human workers. Instead of dedicating human effort to these standardized processes, organizations are redesigning roles so that people focus on strategic activities, complex problem solving, and creative collaboration. For example, rather than inspecting every manufactured component manually, quality-control specialists now oversee automated vision systems, analyze exception reports, and refine inspection parameters to address novel defects.

This evolution gives rise to hybrid positions that blend technical oversight with domain expertise. Maintenance technicians, for instance, must understand both mechanical systems and the analytics platforms that predict equipment failures, allowing them to intervene proactively when anomalies arise. In customer service, agents collaborate with AI-driven chatbots: bots handle common inquiries and route complex issues to human representatives who can exercise empathy and nuanced judgment. These hybrid workflows require workers to develop digital fluency—interpreting machine outputs, adjusting parameters, and ensuring that automated processes align with ethical and operational standards.

New job categories will also emerge around the automated ecosystem itself. Roles such as robot coordinators, data curators, and AI ethics officers will become critical as organizations scale their use of intelligent systems. Robot coordinators program collaborative robots ("cobots"), ensure safe human-robot interactions, and optimize task flows on the factory floor. Data curators maintain the quality of datasets used to train machine-learning models, preventing bias and ensuring reliability. AI ethics officers establish guidelines for responsible algorithmic decision-making, monitor compliance, and investigate unintended consequences of automation.

The structure of work will further evolve toward project-based and outcome-oriented models. Rather than static job descriptions, organizations will form dynamic teams that assemble for specific initiatives—such as launching a new product or responding to supply-chain disruptions—and then disband upon completion. Performance metrics will shift from hours worked to outcomes achieved, fostering agility and innovation. Workers will need adaptability and a growth mindset, continually updating skills and moving fluidly between assignments as projects evolve.

Geography will become less of a barrier as remote management of automated operations gains traction. Control centers can monitor fleets of autonomous vehicles, manage logistics hubs, or coordinate distributed robotic systems from anywhere with an internet connection. This trend will open opportunities for talent in regions previously excluded from high-tech industries, while challenging local workforces to acquire complementary skills.

In essence, automation will redefine jobs by elevating human contributions to areas where creativity, critical thinking, and interpersonal skills are paramount, while entrusting machines with precision, scale, and repetitive tasks. Organizations and workers who embrace this partnership—investing in upskilling, redesigning roles around human-machine collaboration, and fostering adaptability—will unlock greater productivity, innovation, and resilience in the rapidly evolving world of work.

Chapter 9
Redefining Job Security

In an era defined by rapid technological change and shifting employment models, the concept of job security is being reimagined. Traditional long-term roles with fixed schedules and employer-provided benefits are giving way to more flexible arrangements, including short-term contracts, freelance projects, and hybrid work structures. As organizations prioritize agility and cost-efficiency, workers increasingly navigate portfolios of assignments rather than single employer relationships. This shift challenges assumptions about stability but also opens new avenues for autonomy and career growth.

For many, the gig economy offers unparalleled freedom to choose projects, set schedules, and diversify income streams. Yet without guaranteed hours or company-sponsored benefits, gig workers face unpredictable earnings and gaps in health coverage, retirement savings, and paid leave. To thrive amid this uncertainty, individuals and platforms alike are developing mechanisms to foster stability. Some marketplaces offer income smoothing programs, advance payments, or minimum-earnings guarantees, while cooperatives and unions are exploring portable benefit models that decouple healthcare and retirement from specific employers.

Financial resilience in this new landscape depends on proactive planning. Gig workers must build emergency savings, manage irregular cash flows, and secure affordable insurance through government exchanges or specialized providers. Hybrid employment models—combining part-time staff roles with freelance work—can balance the predictability of traditional wages with the flexibility of contract projects. Employers, recognizing the importance of worker well-being, are experimenting with stipends for health benefits, contributions to retirement accounts, and access to co-working spaces, blurring the lines between full-time and contingent labor.

Ultimately, redefining job security means embracing a broader definition of stability—one that goes beyond tenure and paychecks to include financial planning, access to benefits, and a diversified portfolio of work relationships. By building support systems for gig and hybrid workers, fostering continuous skill development, and creating new pooling arrangements for benefits, both individuals and organizations can cultivate a resilient workforce capable of weathering economic fluctuations and technological disruption. In this evolving employment landscape, security lies not in the permanence of a single role, but in the adaptability, resourcefulness, and collective structures that underpin modern careers.

Moving Away from Traditional Job Models

Over the past two decades, traditional job models—characterized by full-time, long-term employment with a single organization—have given way to more fluid arrangements driven by technological, economic, and cultural forces. Historically, a typical career path involved joining a company straight out of school, climbing a well-defined internal ladder, and retiring with a pension funded by employer contributions. Work was anchored to a physical location, schedules were fixed, and benefits such as healthcare, paid leave, and 401(k) matching formed an implicit compact between employer and employee.

Today, many of these assumptions no longer hold. Global competition and rapid innovation have intensified pressure on businesses to remain agile and cost-efficient. Rather than maintaining large, permanent headcounts, companies increasingly rely on contingent labor—contractors, freelancers, and project-based teams—that can be scaled up or down in response to demand. This shift reduces fixed labor costs and provides access to specialized skills on a temporary basis, but it also dissolves the lifetime job guarantee once provided by large employers.

A parallel cultural evolution prioritizes autonomy, purpose, and work-life integration. Younger generations—Millennials and Gen Z—place a higher value on meaningful, passion-driven work and the freedom to design their own schedules. The rise of remote and hybrid work models further erodes the need for central offices, enabling teams to collaborate from anywhere. As a result, geographical boundaries have blurred: talent in Bangalore can join a Silicon Valley startup without relocating, and a marketing strategist in São Paulo can deliver campaigns for clients in London.

Portfolio careers—where individuals combine multiple income streams through part-time jobs, consulting gigs, freelance projects, and even entrepreneurial ventures—have become common. Workers curate their own "employer" mix to balance stability with variety, often supplementing a base salary with project fees or passive income from digital products. This diversification mitigates risk: if one client or sector slows down, other engagements can sustain earnings.

Traditional benefits models are also being reimagined. Portable benefits platforms and professional associations are emerging to provide healthcare, retirement savings, and liability insurance to independent workers. Some governments and organizations are exploring universal or sector-based benefit pools that decouple access to social protections from any single employer.

Ultimately, moving away from traditional job models reflects a broader shift in how work, value, and security are defined. While permanent roles still exist—especially in regulated industries—the modern employment landscape prizes flexibility, continuous learning, and adaptability. Success now depends on one's ability to navigate a mosaic of engagements, cultivate a personal brand, and continuously update skills, rather than rely on tenure and hierarchy. In this dynamic era, career resilience is built through diversification and lifelong development rather than allegiance to a single employer.

Building Stability in the Gig Economy

Building stability in the gig economy requires both individual strategies and systemic innovations that mitigate the inherent volatility of freelance and contract work. At the personal level, gig workers can smooth income fluctuations by diversifying their client base and service offerings. Rather than relying on a single platform or project type, successful freelancers often balance short-term "quick win" assignments with longer-term retainer contracts, which provide a predictable revenue stream. Setting tiered pricing—offering basic, standard, and premium packages—enables workers to capture higher fees for more comprehensive deliverables, while entry-level offerings help maintain a steady flow of smaller jobs.

Financial resilience also hinges on disciplined money management. Establishing an emergency fund that covers at least three to six months of expenses protects against lean periods. Automating savings—such as routing a fixed percentage of every paycheck into a high-yield account—ensures that buffers grow over time. Leveraging budgeting apps designed for irregular incomes can help gig workers track cash flow, forecast upcoming obligations, and adjust spending dynamically.

Beyond personal practices, platforms are increasingly introducing mechanisms to bolster stability. Income-smoothing programs, for instance, provide advances on pending invoices based on a worker's historical earnings, cushioning the gap between project milestones and final payments. Minimum-earnings guarantees pledge a baseline hourly rate or weekly stipend in exchange for meeting participation thresholds, ensuring that active users receive a floor of compensation. Some gig marketplaces experiment with community-funded insurance pools, where small fees from each transaction build a reserve that covers medical claims or unemployment benefits when needed.

Collective approaches are also gaining traction. Cooperatives of freelancers can band together to bid on larger contracts that individual members couldn't tackle alone, sharing both risks and rewards. By pooling revenue, these co-ops can negotiate group health plans, retirement accounts, and training subsidies, approximating the benefit structures of traditional employment. Worker associations and advocacy groups lobby for portable benefits—schemes where contributions toward healthcare or pensions follow the individual rather than the employer—making it possible to accumulate coverage across multiple gigs.

Education and peer mentorship strengthen stability by accelerating skill development and fostering community support. Online forums, local meetups, and virtual coworking sessions allow freelancers to share best practices on pricing, negotiation, and client management. Access to on-demand training modules helps workers pivot into higher-demand specialties, increasing their ability to command premium rates.

Ultimately, building stability in the gig economy requires a multi-pronged approach: disciplined financial planning at the individual level; platform features like advances, guarantees, and pooled benefits; and collective action through cooperatives and portable benefit models. By combining these tactics, gig workers can transform an unpredictable landscape into one that offers both flexibility and a dependable foundation for long-term prosperity.

Financial Security and Health Benefits for Gig Workers

Gig workers often trade the stability of traditional employment for flexibility, but this freedom can come at the cost of financial security and access to health benefits. To bridge this gap, individuals and platforms are pioneering solutions that mirror employer-sponsored packages.

Building Financial Resilience

Without guaranteed paychecks, gig workers must proactively manage irregular income streams. Establishing an emergency fund—ideally covering three to six months of living expenses—provides a buffer against lean periods. Automated savings tools, such as Acorns or Qapital, can round up earnings and divert small amounts into dedicated accounts. For retirement, self-employed professionals can leverage tax-advantaged vehicles: SEP IRAs allow contributions up to 25% of net earnings (capped at $66,000 for 2023), while Solo 401(k)s enable higher combined employee and employer contributions (up to $66,000 plus a $7,500 catch-up for those over 50). These accounts not only build long-term security but also reduce taxable income.

Accessing Health Coverage

Healthcare represents one of the biggest expense challenges for independent workers. The Affordable Care Act's marketplaces offer tiered plans with income-based subsidies, making premiums more affordable for many gig earners. Specialized brokers and apps—such as Stride Health and Catch—aggregate marketplace options and tax tools, guiding users through enrollment and helping calculate deductible savings. Some platforms partner with insurers to offer group-rate discounts; for example, freelancer cooperatives or professional associations negotiate lower premiums for members. Telehealth services, like Maven Clinic or Roman, provide subscription-based care for common needs—mental health, women's health, and men's health—at a fraction of traditional costs.

Platform-Driven Benefit Innovations

Major gig platforms recognize that benefits can boost worker retention and satisfaction. Companies such as Lyft and Instacart have introduced "driver hubs" offering access to low-cost accident insurance, occupational accident coverage, and discounts on vision or dental plans. Income-smoothing programs advance a portion of projected earnings, reducing cash-flow volatility. Some apps automatically calculate and set aside estimated taxes, ensuring compliance and preventing year-end shocks.

Policy and Collective Models

On the policy front, proposals like portable benefits accounts envision contributions from multiple gig employers aggregated into individual benefit pools. California's Assembly Bill 5 and similar legislation in other jurisdictions aim to reclassify certain gig workers as employees, granting them access to minimum wage, unemployment insurance, and employer-sponsored benefits. Meanwhile, freelancer unions and cooperatives form collective bargaining units that secure group health plans, negotiate maternity benefits, and pool resources for paid sick leave.

By combining disciplined personal finance strategies, marketplace tools, platform partnerships, and emerging policy frameworks, gig workers can assemble a robust safety net. While the employment landscape continues to evolve, these approaches ensure that autonomy does not come at the expense of essential financial and health protections.

Chapter 10
Leadership in a Remote World

Leading teams in a world where colleagues may span continents and time zones demands a fresh approach grounded in trust, clarity, and intentional connection. As physical offices give way to home workstations and co-working spaces, managers can no longer rely on casual hallway conversations or visible presence to gauge engagement and progress. Instead, they must establish clear expectations around goals, deliverables, and response times—articulated through well-defined workflows and shared project dashboards. By focusing on outcomes rather than hours logged, leaders empower individuals to organize their days around deep work and personal rhythms, fostering autonomy while maintaining alignment with team objectives.

Sustaining a cohesive culture across virtual boundaries requires deliberate rituals and touchpoints. Regular "all-hands" video gatherings, informal coffee-break calls, and virtual team-building activities help recreate the spontaneity of in-office interactions. Celebrating milestones—whether project launches, birthdays, or "wins of the week"—reinforces shared identity and recognizes contributions. Leaders also model vulnerability and authenticity, sharing both successes and setbacks to invite open dialogue. When teams feel seen and heard, psychological safety grows, enabling candid feedback and creative collaboration despite physical distance.

Communication barriers are an ever-present challenge in remote environments. Time-zone differences, varying internet quality, and the absence of nonverbal cues can lead to misunderstandings and delays. To overcome these hurdles, effective leaders champion a mix of synchronous and asynchronous channels: video calls for complex discussions and relationship building, chat threads for quick questions and real-time support, and detailed documentation for reference. Establishing "core hours" when everyone is online, alongside clear guidelines on which topics belong in email, chat, or shared documents, reduces noise and keeps conversations focused. Encouraging concise, context-rich messages and offering training on virtual-meeting etiquette further sharpens team communication.

Ultimately, leadership in a remote world hinges on empathy, adaptability, and proactive connection. By setting transparent processes, nurturing digital culture, and tailoring communication methods to team needs, leaders can guide distributed teams toward high performance and lasting engagement—no matter where each member happens to log in.

Managing Remote Teams Effectively

Effectively managing remote teams begins with establishing clear expectations and defining success metrics that focus on outcomes rather than hours logged. From the outset, leaders should collaborate with team members to set specific, measurable goals and agree on priorities for each sprint or project cycle. Documenting these objectives in a shared workspace—using tools like project boards or collaborative documents—ensures that everyone understands responsibilities and deadlines, reducing confusion and the need for constant check-ins.

Trust is foundational in a remote environment. Managers must give team members autonomy to choose when and where they work, based on agreed core hours and deliverables. This means resisting the urge to micromanage and instead checking progress through regular status updates and milestone reviews. By framing conversations around achievements and roadblocks, leaders demonstrate respect for each individual's workflow while remaining available to address challenges or reallocate resources.

Communication norms are critical to prevent misunderstandings across time zones and diverse working styles. Teams should decide collectively which platforms suit different purposes—real-time discussion platforms for brainstorming or urgent questions, asynchronous channels for feedback and documentation, and video calls for relationship building or complex discussions. Establishing guidelines around response times helps everyone know when to expect answers, which both reduces anxiety and empowers individuals to plan focused work blocks without constant interruptions.

Regular one-on-one meetings create space for personalized support and development. These check-ins should balance project updates with conversations about workload, career goals, and well-being. In the absence of office proximity, informal interactions can easily fall away, so scheduling periodic "coffee chats" or virtual team lunches fosters camaraderie and helps managers pick up on nonverbal cues about morale or burnout.

Investing in the right technology also streamlines management. Project management software with built-in analytics can surface patterns in task completion, highlight potential bottlenecks, and flag overdue items before they escalate. Shared calendars with visibility into time zones and availability statuses prevent scheduling conflicts and respect personal boundaries. Ensuring that everyone has reliable hardware, secure network access, and training on new tools removes technical barriers that could derail productivity.

Finally, continuous feedback loops drive improvement. At the end of each cycle, teams should conduct brief retrospectives to celebrate successes, identify pain points, and propose actionable changes. By iterating on processes rather than clinging to rigid routines, remote teams evolve practices that suit their unique dynamics and grow more resilient over time. In this way, effective remote management becomes a cycle of trust, clarity, and collaborative refinement—enabling distributed teams to achieve high performance and sustained engagement.

Building a Strong Company Culture Online

Building a strong company culture online starts with articulating clear, shared values that guide every interaction. Leaders must communicate a compelling mission and set of principles from day one—whether through a digital handbook, interactive webinars, or bite-sized videos—so that employees know not only what the organization does but why it matters. Embedding these values into virtual onboarding processes reinforces the company's identity: new hires participate in welcome ceremonies over video conference, meet mentors in small "buddy" groups, and complete guided exercises that connect their roles to the broader mission.

Rituals and routines help translate in-office camaraderie into the digital realm. Regular virtual all-hands meetings provide a platform for leadership to share successes, priorities, and strategic direction. Informal "coffee roulette" pairings randomly connect employees across teams for casual conversation, while themed chat channels (for hobbies, wellness, or gratitude) foster social bonds. Building "watercooler" moments into the calendar prevents isolation and encourages spontaneous collaboration, even when colleagues are continents apart.

Recognition and celebration are central to reinforcing desired behaviors. Public shout-outs during team calls, digital badges awarded through collaboration platforms, and peer-nominated awards boost morale and demonstrate that contributions are noticed. Personal milestones—birthdays, work anniversaries, project launches—can be marked with virtual celebrations, small care-package deliveries, or company-wide shout-out emails, signaling that the organization values individuals as people, not just as performers.

Open communication channels underpin trust within a remote workforce. Establishing norms around responsiveness—such as specific windows for synchronous discussion and guidelines for asynchronous updates—reduces ambiguity. Leaders who model vulnerability and transparency by sharing both wins and setbacks cultivate psychological safety, encouraging employees to voice concerns and propose bold ideas. Anonymous feedback tools and regular pulse surveys help gauge sentiment and identify cultural blind spots before they become problems.

Professional development and mentorship programs reinforce an investment in people. Virtual learning sessions, micro-learning modules, and cross-functional project rotations signal that the organization prioritizes growth alongside performance. Pairing seasoned employees with newcomers in structured mentorship relationships accelerates integration and passes on cultural norms. Offering flexible "focus weeks" for learning and experimentation encourages continuous improvement and aligns with a culture of curiosity.

Finally, inclusive practices ensure that culture resonates across diverse geographies and backgrounds. Scheduling events at rotating times, providing closed-captioning on calls, and celebrating a range of holidays acknowledges the global nature of a remote team. Ensuring equitable access to resources—home-office stipends, mental-health services, or ergonomic equipment—demonstrates a commitment to employee well-being. By weaving these elements together, organizations can build a resilient, cohesive culture that thrives online, driving engagement, collaboration, and a shared sense of purpose.

Overcoming Communication Barriers in Virtual Teams

Virtual teams face unique communication barriers that can hinder collaboration, productivity, and morale. Time-zone differences often mean team members are not online simultaneously, delaying feedback and creating "follow-the-sun" handoffs that can fragment context. To address this, teams should establish core overlap hours—brief windows when everyone is expected to be available for synchronous discussion—while reserving the rest of the day for asynchronous work. Shared calendars with clearly marked availability help coordinate meetings and set expectations around response times.

The absence of nonverbal cues in text-based channels can lead to misunderstandings and unintended tone. A concise message may come off as curt, or a joke may not land as intended. To mitigate this, teams should adopt a mix of communication modalities: video calls for complex, relationship-building conversations; voice messages for tone and nuance; and written summaries afterward to ensure clarity. Encouraging the use of emojis or reaction icons in chat tools offers a quick way to convey empathy or agreement without lengthy replies.

Technology can also be a barrier: unreliable internet connections, unfamiliar platforms, or software glitches disrupt the flow of information. Providing team members with clear onboarding to collaboration tools—along with guidelines for file naming, version control, and folder structures—reduces friction. Maintaining a central, well-organized knowledge base (such as a Wiki or shared drive) ensures that everyone can find critical documents and project updates without hunting through scattered channels.

Cultural and language differences amplify communication challenges. Idioms, humor, or references familiar in one locale may confuse others. Fostering cultural awareness through diversity training and encouraging questions when something isn't understood helps build mutual respect. Teams can rotate "spotlight" sessions where members share local customs or work norms, deepening cross-cultural empathy and strengthening personal bonds.

Information overload is another common pitfall. With multiple chat channels, email threads, and project boards, crucial messages can get buried. Establishing clear guidelines—such as specifying which topics belong in email versus chat, using consistent subject tags, and setting channel hierarchies—helps filter noise. Regular "communication hygiene" sessions, where the team reviews and archives outdated channels or documents, keep the workspace lean and navigable.

Finally, cultivating a culture of feedback ensures continuous improvement. Retrospectives focused on communication—asking what went well, what stalled, and what might change—surface pain points and generate actionable solutions. Leaders should model vulnerability by acknowledging their own mishaps and encouraging teammates to share when they feel left out or confused. By combining structured protocols, diverse communication modes, cultural sensitivity, and ongoing feedback, virtual teams can overcome barriers and achieve seamless, inclusive collaboration.

Chapter 11
The Impact of Automation on Employment

Automation is fundamentally reshaping the employment landscape by taking on tasks once performed exclusively by humans. From industrial robots welding car frames to software bots processing invoices, machines are increasingly capable of handling repetitive, rule-based work with speed and precision. As these technologies spread across sectors—manufacturing, logistics, finance, and even legal services—the question of which roles will remain secure becomes ever more pressing. While some jobs may be fully automated, many others will evolve, blending human skills with machine efficiency to create hybrid functions.

At the same time, automation is not simply a story of job loss. It also gives rise to entirely new roles—robotic maintenance specialists, data curators, and AI ethicists, to name a few—that focus on designing, overseeing, and fine-tuning automated systems. Organizations that embrace this dual reality can reconfigure workflows to capitalize on human strengths—creativity, empathy, strategic insight—while delegating mundane tasks to machines. In doing so, they not only boost productivity but also unlock opportunities for workers to engage in richer, more meaningful work.

Successfully navigating this transition requires a proactive mindset. Workers must anticipate changes, continuously update their skill sets, and seek out training in areas that complement automation technologies. Employers, meanwhile, should invest in reskilling programs, redesign job roles, and foster a culture of lifelong learning. By aligning workforce strategies with technological advancements, both individuals and organizations can adapt to automation not as an external threat but as a catalyst for innovation and growth in the future of work.

Which Jobs Are at Risk of Being Automated?

Jobs characterized by routine, repetitive tasks are most vulnerable to automation. In manufacturing, roles such as assembly-line operators, welders, and quality-control inspectors face high risk as industrial robots and vision systems perform precise, repetitive functions more quickly and consistently than humans. Automated guided vehicles (AGVs) now handle material transport within factories and warehouses, reducing the need for forklift drivers and floor staff.

In the transportation sector, long-haul truck driving is increasingly targeted by autonomous vehicle technologies. Companies are testing self-driving trucks that can operate on highways with minimal human intervention, potentially displacing drivers over multi-hour routes. Similarly, taxi and delivery drivers face encroachment from autonomous cars and drone delivery systems as these technologies mature.

Clerical and administrative roles are another major category at risk. Data-entry clerks, payroll processors, and routine bookkeeping positions are being supplanted by robotic process automation (RPA) software that can log into systems, extract and input data, reconcile records, and generate reports without fatigue or error. Telemarketing and customer-service representatives handling straightforward inquiries also confront replacement by AI-powered chatbots and voice assistants, which can respond instantly to common questions and route complex issues to human agents.

In the retail and hospitality industries, front-line cashier and check-out roles are increasingly automated through self-service kiosks and "just-walk-out" systems that use computer vision to track purchases without human intervention. Fast-food cooks and order-takers may see portions of their jobs automated by robotic fryers, burger-flipping machines, and voice-ordering systems that prepare standard menu items on demand.

Even professional services are not immune. Basic legal work such as document review, contract analysis, and discovery research can be handled by AI algorithms that scan thousands of pages for relevant information. Entry-level accounting tasks—such as invoice review and tax form preparation—are automated by software platforms that apply rule-based logic to financial data. In journalism, automated content-generation tools can produce routine news summaries, sports recaps, and financial reports faster than human writers.

That said, jobs combining routine tasks with human judgment—such as medical laboratory technicians overseeing diagnostic machines or administrative assistants coordinating schedules and travel—will often evolve rather than disappear entirely. In these hybrid roles, workers supervise automated processes, handle exceptions, and provide the interpersonal skills and contextual understanding that machines currently lack. Understanding which jobs are most at risk helps workers and organizations anticipate changes, prioritize reskilling efforts, and reconfigure job designs to integrate automation as a complement, not a replacement, to human talent.

The Potential for New Job Roles in an Automated World

As automation takes over routine tasks, it simultaneously opens doors to a range of new roles centered on the design, oversight, and continuous improvement of intelligent systems. One emerging category is that of automation architects and engineers, professionals who map existing workflows, identify automation opportunities, and build end-to-end solutions. These specialists blend process engineering with software development skills, configuring robotic process automation (RPA) tools, integrating AI models, and ensuring that automated workflows align with business objectives.

Maintaining and optimizing automated systems creates demand for machine-maintenance technicians with hybrid mechanical and digital expertise. On factory floors, these technicians service collaborative robots ("cobots"), update firmware, troubleshoot sensor networks, and liaise with IT teams to ensure uptime. In offices, "bot wranglers" monitor software bots, adjust parameters to handle exceptions, and refine decision rules as business needs evolve. Their role parallels that of traditional IT support but focuses specifically on the health of automation platforms.

As algorithms permeate decision-making, the need for data curators and quality stewards grows. These professionals gather, clean, and label training data for machine-learning models, ensuring that inputs are accurate, representative, and free from harmful bias. They establish data-governance protocols, track lineage, and collaborate with domain experts to interpret anomalies. Without high-quality data, AI systems can produce unreliable or unfair outcomes, making the curator role indispensable.

Ethical oversight and compliance roles will also expand. AI ethicists and algorithmic audit officers develop guidelines to assess fairness, transparency, and privacy implications of automated systems. They conduct impact assessments, review model outputs for discriminatory patterns, and recommend corrective measures. In heavily regulated sectors—finance, healthcare, and government—these specialists work alongside legal teams to ensure that AI deployments meet evolving regulatory standards.

In customer-facing contexts, new hybrid roles blend human empathy with technical fluency. "Digital concierges" and AI trainers teach virtual assistants to understand company-specific language and tone, refining natural-language models through iterative feedback. They handle complex or emotionally sensitive interactions escalated from chatbots, while feeding conversational data back into training pipelines to improve bot performance.

Finally, strategy and innovation roles emerge around automation's broader business impact. Automation strategists and digital-transformation consultants advise C-suite leaders on how to balance human and machine labor, redesign organizational structures, and cultivate a culture that embraces continuous improvement. They measure return on automation investments, identify cross-functional automation initiatives, and oversee change-management programs that prepare workforces for new hybrid roles.

Together, these positions reflect a shift from manual execution toward system design, governance, and collaboration with intelligent machines. By focusing on areas where human judgment, creativity, and ethical reasoning are paramount, workers can thrive alongside automation rather than be sidelined by it.

Strategies for Adapting to Automation

Adapting to automation begins with embracing a lifelong learning mindset. As routine tasks become automated, individuals should proactively identify emerging skills that complement machine strengths—such as critical thinking, emotional intelligence, and data literacy. Regularly auditing one's skill set against market trends helps pinpoint gaps: for example, taking online courses in basic programming or process design can prepare workers to configure and collaborate with automated systems. Building a portfolio of project case studies—documenting experiences with new tools, process improvements, or cross-functional collaborations—demonstrates adaptability to employers and clients alike.

Another key strategy is to seek hybrid roles that blend human judgment with machine efficiency. Rather than viewing automation solely as a threat, workers can position themselves as supervisors of bots and robots, troubleshooting exceptions, refining algorithms, and interpreting outputs. For example, customer-service representatives might specialize in handling escalated inquiries that chatbots cannot resolve, while logistics coordinators oversee autonomous vehicles, optimizing routes based on real-time data. By reframing job identities around oversight and exception management, individuals carve out irreplaceable niches in automated environments.

Networking and collaboration also play a vital role. Joining professional communities—both online and in person—exposes individuals to automation best practices and peer-driven advice. Mentorship relationships can accelerate learning curves, as seasoned professionals share insights on emerging tools and industry-specific use cases. Participating in cross-disciplinary teams provides hands-on experience integrating automation into workflows and helps workers learn how to communicate effectively with technical specialists and leadership.

At an organizational level, companies must invest in structured reskilling and upskilling programs. Rather than waiting for automation to displace roles, employers can map current job tasks, identify automation candidates, and then offer targeted training that transitions employees into new positions—such as automation analysts or bot coordinators. Embedding learning opportunities directly into the workday, through micro-learning modules or job rotations, ensures that skill development keeps pace with technological change.

Redesigning jobs around outcomes rather than input hours further aligns human effort with automation. By defining roles through deliverables—such as problem resolution rates or innovation goals—instead of task lists, organizations empower workers to leverage automation tools creatively. This outcome-based approach encourages experimentation, as employees can choose which technologies best support their objectives.

Finally, policymakers and industry leaders can smooth the transition by fostering portable benefits and modular certification systems. When workers move between roles or employers, portable credentials—earned through short courses or project portfolios—verify their automation-related competencies. Portable benefit schemes, decoupled from single employers, ensure that gig workers and contract professionals maintain access to training subsidies and social protections throughout their careers. Together, these individual, organizational, and systemic strategies create an ecosystem where workers are prepared to thrive alongside automation rather than be displaced by it.

Chapter 12
Ethics and Regulation in the Future of Work

As technology redefines the workplace, ethical considerations and regulatory frameworks must evolve in tandem to ensure that progress benefits all stakeholders. The rapid deployment of artificial intelligence and automation raises questions about fairness, transparency, and accountability: when algorithms influence hiring, performance evaluations, or resource allocation, biases baked into data can perpetuate discrimination or amplify inequality. Ensuring that AI systems are designed and audited with ethical guardrails—such as explainable decision-making, bias mitigation protocols, and meaningful human oversight—is essential to uphold workers' rights and public trust.

Parallel challenges emerge in the gig economy, where flexible, platform-mediated work offers autonomy but often falls outside traditional labor protections. Independent contractors may lack minimum-wage guarantees, paid leave, or social safety nets. Ambiguities in worker classification spark legal battles over whether gig workers should receive employee benefits or remain contractors. Crafting clear legal definitions and standards—addressing issues like collective bargaining, unemployment coverage, and liability—

becomes critical as more people rely on on-demand platforms for income.

Governments around the world are experimenting with policies to balance innovation and protection. Some jurisdictions mandate algorithmic impact assessments for high-stakes AI applications, while others require platform companies to contribute to portable benefits funds that follow workers from gig to gig. Progressive labor laws introduce minimum earnings guarantees or extend unemployment insurance to contingent workers. At the same time, international dialogue on data privacy, intellectual property, and cross-border employment seeks to harmonize rules in an increasingly global labor market.

Navigating this complex landscape requires collaboration among technologists, employers, regulators, and worker representatives. Ethical frameworks must inform design and procurement of automated systems, while legal reforms safeguard those in non-traditional roles. By aligning technological innovation with robust protections—grounded in fairness, transparency, and social responsibility—the future of work can harness new efficiencies without sacrificing human dignity or equitable opportunity.

The Ethical Implications of AI and Automation

The ethical implications of AI and automation extend far beyond technical capabilities, touching on issues of fairness, accountability, privacy, and the very definition of human work.

Bias and Fairness

AI systems learn from historical data, which often reflects societal prejudices. If left unchecked, these biases can become embedded in decision-making tools—whether in hiring algorithms that screen resumes, credit models that determine loan approvals, or predictive-policing systems that allocate law-enforcement resources. Ensuring fairness requires rigorous bias detection and mitigation: diverse teams must audit training datasets, implement fairness metrics, and continuously monitor outcomes to prevent disparate impacts on protected groups.

Transparency and Explainability

Many AI models—particularly deep-learning networks—operate as "black boxes," producing high-accuracy predictions without clear explanations of how they arrived at their conclusions. In domains like healthcare and criminal justice, opacity undermines trust and can impede meaningful recourse when errors occur. Ethically deployed AI demands explainable methods that provide human-readable rationales, enabling stakeholders to challenge or verify automated decisions and ensuring that individuals retain agency over processes that affect them.

Accountability and Liability

When an automated system causes harm—such as a misdiagnosis, wrongful arrest, or vehicle collision—assigning responsibility can become murky. Developers, deployers, and end users may share liability in complex ways. Ethical frameworks must clarify accountability pathways, mandating human-in-the-loop oversight, establishing standards for rigorous testing, and requiring transparent incident-response protocols. Regulatory bodies may need to define liability thresholds and enforce compliance through audits and penalties.

Privacy and Surveillance

Automation often relies on large-scale data collection—from biometric scanners to location trackers—that can infringe on individual privacy. AI-driven surveillance systems may erode civil liberties, normalizing constant monitoring in workplaces and public spaces. Ethically guided design limits data collection to legitimate purposes, implements robust anonymization techniques, and obtains informed consent. Strong data-governance policies and encryption safeguards help balance innovation with respect for personal boundaries.

Impact on Work and Human Dignity

Automation can eliminate repetitive, dangerous, or tedious tasks, but it also risks devaluing human labor and displacing workers en masse. Ethical deployment involves designing technology as a collaborator rather than a replacer—freeing humans for creative, strategic, and interpersonal activities while supporting displaced workers through reskilling programs and social safety nets. Organizations must weigh efficiency gains against the societal obligation to preserve meaningful employment and human dignity.

Long-Term Societal Effects

Beyond immediate applications, advanced AI raises philosophical questions about autonomy, self-determination, and social cohesion. Will pervasive automation concentrate wealth in the hands of a few technology owners? Could AI-driven content generation erode the value of human creativity? Addressing these concerns calls for inclusive public dialogue, interdisciplinary research, and policy frameworks that distribute both the benefits and responsibilities of AI equitably.

In sum, the ethical implications of AI and automation demand proactive stewardship—combining technical safeguards, transparent governance, and a commitment to human-centered values—to ensure that emerging technologies uplift society without compromising fairness, privacy, or dignity.

Legal Issues Surrounding Gig Work

Gig work exists in a legal gray zone that challenges traditional labor laws and raises questions about worker classification, benefits entitlement, and liability. The most prominent issue is determining whether gig workers are "employees" entitled to labor protections or "independent contractors" responsible for their own taxes, insurance, and benefits. Courts and regulators worldwide have struggled to apply existing criteria—such as degree of control, financial dependency, and permanence of relationship—to platform-mediated work. Misclassification can deprive workers of minimum wage guarantees, overtime pay, unemployment insurance, and worker's compensation.

Worker classification disputes have sparked major litigation. In the United States, Uber and Lyft drivers have sued for employee status under federal and state labor laws, citing platforms' control over pricing, performance standards, and deactivation policies. Similar cases in the United Kingdom and Europe have led some courts to grant gig workers benefits like holiday pay and pension contributions. Conversely, platforms argue that flexible scheduling and the ability to set rates demonstrate independence. Legislative responses—such as California's Assembly Bill 5—attempt to codify stricter criteria for contractor status, but have faced pushback and carve-outs that dilute their impact.

Beyond classification, gig workers often lack access to essential protections. Without employee status, they cannot claim paid sick leave, family leave, or occupational health and safety coverage. This gap became acute during the COVID-19 pandemic, when many drivers and delivery workers faced exposure risks without guaranteed income or paid medical leave. Some platforms introduced hardship funds or limited benefits, but these measures vary widely in generosity and eligibility, leaving many workers unprotected.

Liability is another complex legal area. When a gig worker causes an accident or injury—such as a collision while driving for a ride-hail service—determining whether the platform shares responsibility depends on the jurisdiction and the level of control the platform exerts. Some courts have held platforms vicariously liable when they dictate routing, pricing, or performance standards; others have treated them as mere intermediaries, shifting liability to individual contractors and their personal insurance.

Data privacy and algorithmic transparency present additional concerns. Gig platforms collect extensive information on worker performance, customer ratings, and location tracking. Workers may face deactivation or "algorithmic management" without clear recourse or explanation. Legal frameworks such as the European Union's GDPR mandate transparency and the right to human intervention, but enforcement in the gig context remains uneven.

Finally, collective bargaining rights are in flux. Independent contractors historically lack union protection, yet gig workers have organized strikes and lobbied for sector-wide agreements. Some jurisdictions are exploring novel frameworks—like "third-party" associations or portable benefit funds—that grant limited collective negotiation rights without full employee status.

Navigating these legal complexities requires cohesive policy responses: clear classification rules, portable benefits decoupled from single employers, liability frameworks that reflect platform influence, and protections for privacy and algorithmic fairness. Only through balanced reforms can gig work retain its flexibility while ensuring fundamental labor rights and social safety nets.

Government Policies for Protecting Workers in the Future

Governments around the world are exploring innovative policy frameworks to ensure that workers remain protected as traditional employment models evolve. One key approach is the development of portable benefits systems that decouple health insurance, retirement savings, and paid leave from a single employer. Under these schemes, contributions are pooled into individual worker accounts, funded proportionally by each engaging platform or client. Regardless of whether a person works for one company or multiple gig apps, they maintain continuous access to social protections—a model already piloted in parts of Europe and under consideration in several U.S. states.

Another emerging policy area is the formal recognition of contingent workforce registries. Rather than treating freelancers and contractors as entirely separate from employees, governments can require platforms and hiring entities to register gig workers with a centralized labor office. This registry enables tracking of total earnings, contribution of social security taxes, and aggregation of benefits eligibility thresholds. It also gives labor authorities clearer visibility into labor market dynamics, helping them set minimum-earnings floors and negotiate sector-wide agreements that protect all workers in an industry.

Algorithmic transparency regulations are gaining traction as well. Knowing that automated systems now determine assignments, rates, and deactivation, several jurisdictions are mandating that platforms disclose key parameters of their matching and rating algorithms. Workers must be informed when they have been "deactivated" or penalized by an automated process, with a right to human review. Such policies help prevent unfair or opaque decision-making and strengthen worker trust in platform operations.

To bolster income stability, policymakers are considering a form of universal basic income (UBI) or earnings guarantee for all workers. Instead of tying income support solely to unemployment benefits, a modest baseline payment—adjusted for cost of living—would ensure that no individual's earnings fall below a poverty threshold. This safety net complements targeted retraining grants, which fund skills development in high-demand fields like data analytics, cybersecurity, and AI ethics. By providing vouchers or tax credits for approved educational programs, governments can help displaced workers transition into new roles.

Finally, labor laws are being updated to grant limited collective bargaining rights to non-employee workers. In some countries, professional associations or designated gig-worker councils can negotiate minimum rates, dispute-resolution processes, and working-condition standards on behalf of their members, even without full employment status. Coupled with anti-monopsony enforcement—crackdowns on dominant platforms that can set unfair terms—these measures aim to rebalance power between individual workers and large digital intermediaries.

Through these policy innovations—portable benefits, workforce registries, algorithmic transparency, baseline income guarantees, and collective-negotiation frameworks—governments can create a more inclusive future of work that values flexibility without sacrificing security.

www.ingramcontent.com/pod-product-compliance
Lightning Source LLC
LaVergne TN
LVHW051035070526
838201LV00009B/204